4 –

The
Dangers of
Contemplative
Prayer

Pacific Press® Publishing Association
Nampa, Idaho
Oshawa, Ontario, Canada
www.pacificpress.com

Hart Research Center

Cover design resources from iStockphoto.com and dreamstime.com
Inside design by Howard A. Peth

Copyright © 2012 by
Pacific Press® Publishing Association
Printed in the United States of America
All rights reserved.

Additional copies of this book are available by calling toll-free 1-800-765-6955 or by visiting http://www.adventistbookcenter.com.

ISBN 13: 978-0-8163-2689-1
ISBN 10: 0-8163-2689-4

12 13 14 15 16 • 5 4 3 2 1

This book is dedicated
to all those who
TREASURE TRUTH,
who SEARCH for it, and,
having FOUND it,
joyfully SHARE it
with others.

FOREWORD

Many are asking, "What's all the fuss about 'Spiritual Formation' and the buzz about 'Contemplative Prayer'? Sure seems to be OK with me! What could possibly be wrong or bad about 'Spiritual Formation'—it sounds like sanctification! And haven't we been told that we should spend 'a thoughtful hour each day in contemplation of the life of Christ?'"

Precisely, and that is part of the problem!

Howard Peth is looking at the recent phenomenon called "emerging," or "new spirituality," that is emphasizing Spiritual Formation and Contemplative Prayer sweeping through almost all Protestant churches everywhere—with his mouth wide open and his brain in overdrive!

He sees time-honored biblical words and concepts that have been understood for two thousand years being hijacked into twenty-first-century meanings! Same words with new meanings *that seem* not only fresh but marvelously believable in a day when old rules and traditions have been junked by postmodern thinking.

So what does all this new way of looking at "old" biblical concepts mean as we try to pick our way through the huge flood of books, TV talk shows, church services that rattle the "saints," *etc.*—all of which is programmed to change the way young and old think about what God is like and how He wants us to think about Him.

Professor Peth is the first to admit that not all is well in some of our church worship programs—that some are boring and not connecting with either the young or the older. But the answer is not in throwing out biblical principles regarding the kind of God running this universe. Rather, we should *look again* at what those principles really are that "turned the world upside down" in the first century A.D.

At the same time, we must face head-on what has been predicted for these last days: "Perilous [strong word] times will come: for men will be lovers of themselves . . . having a form of godliness but denying its power . . . when they will not endure sound doctrine, but according to their own desires, because they have itching ears, they will heap up for themselves teachers; and they will turn their ears away from the truth, and be turned aside to fables" —**2 Timothy 3:1–4:4.**

Those prophetic words from the pen of Paul—as sobering as they are—seem to be growing truer and truer every day! Both professed Christians and the ungodly are now hardly distinguishable. Satan is delighted that his age-old seductive weapon of *spiritualism,* formerly forbidden absolutely by Christian leaders, is now seeping more and more into evangelical Protestant churches. Under the influence of the so-called New Age—which never died out—seekers are captivated by listening to "spirit voices" as they trust ancient mysticism in a fashionably modern dress!

In other words, the prophetic radar screen is becoming clearer by the day! Before you finish reading this small volume, you will see the "blips" on that screen as Professor Peth highlights them for you. I promise you that you will see exactly the kind of world predicted, virtually word for word.

One way to test the alluring appeal of New Spirituality and those featuring "spiritual formation" and "contemplative prayer" is to ask certain questions:

1. What is said about the future of this world—is it a world united in peace or a world in the turmoil of the seven last plagues and the return of Jesus?

2. Who is the Christ they want to "experience"—is He the Resurrected Lord of Heaven and Earth, still in human form, waiting to return to earth, or is "He" the God-consciousness that resides within each and every one of us and who can be "found" by contemplation?

3. What is the role or purpose of the Bible—is it God's message with His plan to forgive and empower its readers, or is it a collection of religious history recalling how others "experienced" their God-consciousness?

4. In presenting the "spiritual formation" emphasis as something now needed in the Christian church, what kind of books are being used as study materials?

In these pages, you will see more clearly how appealing and clever "Satanic witchery" continues to capture truth-seekers. You will follow the threads of Satanic charm that unfortunately have fascinated men and women for centuries, and by God's grace you'll be warned against them.

Herbert Edgar Douglass, ThD
Lincoln, California

Author's Preface

Sooner or later, almost everyone wants to get closer to God. This impulse seems to be a part of our instinctive human make-up. We find it in the mystics among the Hindus and Buddhists, and in the Sufis among the Muslims. This natural, in-born desire has for centuries been traced among Catholic monks and nuns, and even among Quakers. I dare say even hard-core atheists and everyday doubters, underneath it all, and in their quiet times of reflection, feel an indescribable longing to draw close to the Supreme Being—*if* He momentarily exists in their conscious world.

In more recent times, sophisticated moderns in Protestant evangelical churches have attended weekend workshops or even week-long retreats to receive training that promises to satisfy this universal hunger, this longing to go into God's "presence"—and even hear His voice speaking to them.

In just the last few years, literally thousands of Christians—pastors, youth leaders, and ordinary believers—have paid large sums of money to learn techniques that take them into "the Silence" where—they are told—they can hear God's voice. *And in "the Silence," they really **DO** hear "spirit voices" speaking to them directly and personally!* It's quite an experience, a very seductive experience.

But Christian leaders—who see their flocks being deceived, misled, and exploited by this new craze—see it as diabolically dangerous, a threat not only to every *individual involved and ensnared*, but also to *Christ's church as a whole!*

Why do they come to this conclusion? Is it *wrong* to want to be *closer* to God? To *feel* close to Him? Or even somehow to sense the Lord *speaking* to us? Of course not! It's not only natural, it's spiritually beneficial, and something the Lord Himself desires, as our loving heavenly Father. And our dear Savior who gave His very life for us, said with tears in His voice: "O Jerusalem, Jerusalem! . . . How often I wanted to gather your children together, as a hen gathers her chicks under her wings, but you were not willing!" —**Matthew 23:37.**

So the Lord wants—and eagerly waits—to see this God-given impulse manifest itself in our lives. But . . . this thing which is the subject of the book you're now reading, this thing called "Contemplative Prayer," is absolutely ***the wrong way*** to satisfy the hunger to get closer to God!

Let me explain briefly before you go deeper into these pages. Contemplative Prayer is not difficult to learn. Interested students can be taught the basic idea in thirty minutes or less—although they are told to "practice" it regularly and faithfully twice a day, every day, for twenty minutes or more each morning, and twenty minutes or more each night before retiring.

But students are also told that to enter "the Silence"—which is essential and the whole point of the training—"You must learn to *empty your mind.* You must banish every stray thought, or feeling, or image until you reach the 'center' of your consciousness. Only then will you begin to hear new voices of love and truth—spirit voices that will tell you things you never heard before, never knew before."

When students trying to learn Contemplative Prayer techniques wonder aloud, "How can I possibly 'empty' my mind when it keeps constantly *thinking*—even when I'm trying hard to fall asleep at night?" the answer given is an ancient one—a technique discovered millenniums ago in ancient India by Hindu mystics of the East. Those mystics would tell you what they found: that by saying a syllable, word, or phrase and *repeating* it over and over every time a thought intrudes into your mind you will *finally banish every stray thought* and clear your mind for "the Silence" so you can actually hear the voices of the spirits you're endeavoring to hear.

The word repeated in this manner is called a "mantra" from the ancient Sanskrit language, and the mantras the Hindu mystics used ages ago—and still use today in order to enter the trancelike "Silence"—are the names of their various *Hindu gods.* However, in the Christian churches where Contemplative Prayer is now being taught, they usually change the term "mantra" to "prayer word" and tell the student to choose a Christian name to be repeated, such as "Father" or "Jesus."

But merely changing the terminology from *mantra* to *prayer word* and suggesting the name of a Christian deity instead of a Hindu god or goddess does not change the reality that *the roots and sources of Contemplative Prayer are from the ancient pagan religions of Hinduism and Buddhism.* The inconvenient truth for those who promote Contemplative Prayer is that it is **NOT Christian** at all and **NOT biblical** at all. Much to the contrary, it is condemned by the Lord Jesus in these words from **Matthew 6:7**—"When you pray, *do not use vain repetitions as the heathen do.*"

I have of necessity used the word *mystic* in this Preface, so perhaps I should define its meaning. The *American Heritage Dictionary, Second College Edition*, says this about the word *mystical:* "Of, pertaining to, or stemming from **direct** communion with ultimate reality or God." The Hindu guru, Buddhist priest, African witch doctor, Indian medicine man, or spiritualistic medium/channeler/psychic all believe that they have been blessed with the gift of **direct**, personal contact with the invisible, supernatural world of spiritual Reality—or, as our definition says, "ultimate reality or God."

And they do indeed have direct contact with "spirit voices" that they hear speaking to them personally. They don't get their information *second-hand*, from, say, reading the Bible or listening to an insightful sermon. No, the mystic *believes* he gets his teachings directly from the divine Source. *But what he fails to consider* is that the spirit world—ever since Lucifer's rebellion in heaven, has contained *both* angels *and* demons, good *and* evil, truth *and* error.

And therein lies the danger, as pointed out in this book.

But stop to think for just a moment: *How does God communicate with mankind?* Before the entrance of sin, Adam did enjoy **direct**, open communion with his Maker. But since man separated himself from God by transgression, the plan of redemption has opened another avenue whereby we may still have connection with Heaven. Through His Holy Spirit, God gave revelations to His chosen servants—prophets and apostles—as we read: "Holy men of God spoke as they were moved by the Holy Spirit."—**2 Peter 1:21.**

So those who will, may hear God's voice still speaking to them directly in His written Word, the Bible—which is "God's Love Letter to the Human Race." And as we peruse the pages of His inspired Book, God expects us to use our MINDS. " 'Come now, and let us REASON together,' says the Lord."—**Isaiah 1:18.** Thus the "**mystic** meditation" that tells us to *empty our mind* of every last thought is *poles apart* from the "**Christian** meditation" that God approves, in which we *think deeply* upon lovely themes and *dwell* upon uplifting ideas.

For with our MINDS we enter into a relationship with God. The apostle Paul urges in **Romans 12:2**—"Do not be conformed to this world, but be **transformed** by the **renewing** of your **MIND**, that you may prove what is that good and acceptable and perfect will of God."

As we enter into God's presence through prayer and the study of His Word, the Holy Spirit transforms our *thinking.* Transformed thoughts lead to transformed *behavior,* and then to a new, transformed *life* in Christ.

Before concluding this Preface, I should mention one last feature of today's religious scene, one that is often tied to, and that implements, Contemplative Prayer: "The Emerging Church."

The Emerging Church—sometimes called the "Emergent Church"—is reflective of the trend toward innovation and novelty promoted by spiritual leaders who *"will try anything once,"* as some people say. But it's also a reflection of the fact that <u>church pastors have a hard job:</u> They're pulled in opposite directions by forces that seem to be in conflict with each other.

On the one hand, Christian pastors have sworn to uphold the Word of God and teach its doctrinal truths. On the other hand is the reality that they have to please the congregation, or people won't keep coming back.

Praise the Lord that there are still sincere, faithful pastors devoted to the God-given truths they're called to preach. And they're happy to continue doing that wonderful work in traditional ways without compromise. Others who are equally sincere and dedicated—and who perhaps have had experience in the business world before being called to the ministry—have been more willing to try new, even revolutionary, methods.

You see, leaders in the BUSINESS world don't have that *first* commitment of pastoral work to worry about. So they simply follow the advice of psychologists and advertising geniuses who adhere to the market-driven principle of *"Give the customer what he wants."* All advertising commercials are extremely *market driven.*

In the last few decades, some pastors who were worried about their dwindling flocks looked around and saw the success in the business world of the market-driven principle. A few of them reasoned, "The person in the pew is like the customer in the store—he's *seeking* something." So they did in-depth studies analyzing their church-going seekers in order to determine exactly what they were seeking. And they came up with a blueprint for a "seeker-friendly church" that gave birth to the first Emerging Church.

This seeker-driven principle is based on the premise of *"Give the seeker what he wants."* Never mind what God wants. That first commitment for ministers of the gospel isn't even in the equation. "Doctrine" is virtually a *dirty word* in the Emerging Church. Sermons are replaced by dramatic skits or "the Conversation" in which seekers lounge around in a semi-circle and offer comments on a topic led by a facilitator sitting on a barstool—and everyone's opinion counts, no matter how far-fetched and outrageous.

But we may ask: Are all these radical changes good? Do the *seekers themselves* even know what is best—do they really have enough wisdom to write their own prescription for what ails them? They do sense a real hunger for truth, and they go to a church expecting to be fed and instructed. So is it wise to throw out God's Textbook for the course?

And does the local minister honestly have a legitimate right to revamp, revise, and revolutionize the whole worship experience simply because he thinks the sheep in his flock *belong to him*—or do those sheep *really* belong to Christ, who calls Himself "the Good Shepherd"? —**John 10:11–16.**

Is it safe for a mere man to *change* God's teachings according to his own private inclinations? No! Not when **2 Peter 1:20** says, "Knowing this first, that *no* prophecy of Scripture is of any *private* interpretation," and **Revelation 22:18–19** warns of terrible punishments awaiting "*anyone*" who "adds to" or "takes away from" the words of God.

We should not presume to judge the leaders in the Emerging Church movement. God alone knows their hearts and minds. *They themselves may well be good men* with the **BEST** of **MOTIVES**—a strong, sincere desire to reach the world for Christ—*but their market-driven* **METHODS** *are wrong*.

For the Emerging Church offers us "feel good" churches that are "seeker friendly" and whose middle name is "compromise," where God's Truth is strongly diluted by "dumbing down" the teachings of God's Word.

All this may sound too unbelievable to accept, but I assure you that this watering down of the Christian gospel message is absolutely true today—and it's a *literal fulfillment* of Paul's sad prophecy:

> **2 Timothy 4:3–4** — The time will come when they will not endure sound doctrine, but according to their own desires, because they have itching ears, they will heap up for themselves teachers; and they will turn their ears away from the truth, and be turned aside to fables.

In closing, let me say that what you're about to read is by no means an exhaustive, comprehensive treatment of the subject but is instead *a brief overview* which I hope you'll find "user-friendly."

I must admit that as I was writing the pages that follow, at times I felt impelled by a terrible sense of *urgency* because this subject is *a deadly serious one*. I pray that my message may not offend anyone but instead will awaken all to something absolutely fatal: this "Trojan Horse" which has already stealthily entered the church.

H. A. P.
San Diego, California
October 2011

- Bible texts are from the *New King James Version* unless otherwise noted.

- Titles and pronouns referring to DEITY are capitalized, even in quotations where they were not so printed.

- Emphasis is supplied, even in quotations, to telegraph meaning for instant intelligibility. Subtle nuances are thus made so clear that one can almost hear the author's voice.

- Contractions are freely used to achieve a lighter, more conversational tone in what might otherwise be heavy and bookish. Popular nonfiction presents scholarly facts to the masses, but a serious subject needn't be a solemn one!

THE DANGERS OF CONTEMPLATIVE PRAYER

FOREWORD v
AUTHOR'S PREFACE vii
INTRODUCTION: "Satan Never Sleeps"—The Anatomy of a Heresy .. 14

PART I. Contemplative Prayer: What It Is and How It Works.......19

   A. Mantras, Meditation, and Mysticism.................. 20
   B. Talk About *Repetition!!!*.............................21
   C. Deceptively Switching Labels......................... 22
   D. "The Silence" 23
   E. Trances and Hypnotism, Anyone?.......................25
   F. "Clutching at Straws" in the Scriptures 27
      1. Scripture Text #1: Psalm 46:10.................. 27
      2. Scripture Text #2: Matthew 6:6 29
      3. Scripture Text #3: 1 Kings 19:12 30
   G. Is Contemplative Prayer _REALLY_ an
      Advanced Form of Christian Prayer?............. 31
      1. Is Contemplative Prayer _CHRISTIAN?_ 31
      2. Is Contemplative Prayer _EVEN PRAYER?_ 32
      3. None Need Be Deceived and Misled 34

PART II. Monks and Mystics as ROOTS and SOURCES.............38

   A. Deep Roots in the Roman Catholic Church............. 38
      1. The Desert Fathers ca. 270–500...................... 38
      2. *The Cloud of Unknowing* ca. 1375................... 38
      3. Ignatius of Loyola 1491–1556........................39
      4. Thomas Merton 1915–1968 39
      5. Thomas Keating 1923– 40
      6. Basil Pennington 1931–2005.................... 40
      7. Henri Nouwen 1932–1996.................... 40
      8. Brennan Manning 1930– 41
   B. Earlier Roots in Ancient EASTERN Religions 42
      1. When EAST Meets WEST........................42
      2. CP and TM Are Mystical TWINS! 46
      3. CHART: "Spiritual TWINS" 46

  C. Modern Sources in PROTESTANT Proponents 48
      1. Richard Foster and the Quaker Connection 48
          a. The Quakers' Practice of "the Silence" 50
          b. The Quakers' False Worldview 50
          c. The Quakers' Setting Aside the Bible 51
      2. Dallas Willard 1935–   52
      3. Rick Warren   1954–   52
  D. "THE EMERGING CHURCH" 53
      PERSONAL EXPERIENCE TRUMPS DOCTRINE! 54
      1. Dan Kimball 55
      "Ancient-Future" Worship 55
      2. Robert Webber 1933–2007 55
      "Join the Conversation!" 56
      Multi-Sensory Worship 57
      3. Brian McLaren 1956–   58

PART III. Deadly DANGERS of Contemplative Prayer 60
  A. Your Voluntary *Consent* Is Required 60
  B. Perilous Exposure to Demonic Influence 61
      A Pleasant Mind-Body "Experience" 62
      1. Even Practitioners and Proponents
          ADMIT Its Dangers! 65
      2. The Awful "Alpha" of Mind Control! 69
  C. Undermining the Authority of God's Word 70
      1. *Deliberately Misquoting* Scripture 71
      2. *Downgrading and Denigrating* the Bible 73
  D. Adopting False and Fatal Worldviews 78
      Coming to Terms: Universalism, Monism,
          Pantheism, and Panentheism 78
      Scripture Text #4: Luke 17:21 84
      A Good Rule: "Consider the Context" 84
      "Location, Location, Location!" 86
      A DIVINE PREDICTION COME TRUE! 91
      God Warns Us Against "Seducing Spirits" 92

CONCLUSION: "BELOVED, BELIEVE *NOT* EVERY SPIRIT" 95
      TRUTH AND FALSEHOOD: POLAR OPPOSITES 95

NOTES 98

INTRODUCTION: "SATAN NEVER SLEEPS"
—THE ANATOMY OF A HERESY

God has His faithful people—His sheep—everywhere in this world, and He loves them and cares for them as "the Good Shepherd" that He is. That's what Jesus calls Himself in **John 10:11–16**, where He says also: "The Good Shepherd gives His life for the sheep." And He adds, "My sheep hear My voice, and I know them, and they follow Me," **verse 27.**

But sometimes even the best sheep, who always follow the Shepherd, *hear other voices and become confused;* as Jesus said, "The wolf catches the sheep, and scatters them," **verse 12.** Yet we need not worry, for Jesus—who knows everything about shepherding God's beautiful flock—tells us: "Other sheep I have which are not of this fold; them also I must bring, and *they shall hear My voice;* and there will be one flock and one Shepherd," **verse 16.**

An example of this may be seen in **Acts 6:7,** which says:

> Then the word of God spread, and the number of the disciples multiplied greatly in Jerusalem, and *a great many of the PRIESTS* were obedient to the faith.

Those Jewish priests were good men, sincere men, faithful to what they had all their lives been taught. They had heard "other voices" and followed them. But then, after hearing the voice of the Good Shepherd in the apostles' preaching about the Messiah, they followed Him and "were obedient to the faith." In fact, perhaps the most zealous of all the Jewish leaders was *Saul of Tarsus,* who experienced God's miraculous metamorphosis of conversion to become *Paul, the great apostle to the Gentiles!*

How many today are there—good people, loyal followers of the faith of Jesus all their lives—who may have become confused and misled by "other voices"? Sincerely wanting to do what's right, honestly seeking a closer, more intimate experience with the Lord they love, they've been deceived and seduced. They've innocently followed a way that "seems right" to them.

The Bible puts it this way—twice!—"There is a way that *seems right* to a man, but its end is the way of death," **Proverbs 14:12, 16:25.**

But God wants each and every one of those "sheep" who may have been misled to come *back* to Him—now, before it's too late. He loves them and calls them "*My* sheep" and "*My* people." In **Revelation 18:4** He calls, "*Come out* of her, *My* people"—come out of deception and stop listening to other voices.

It's easy to understand that deception is rampant when we recall that our universe is a battleground, the scene of a great controversy—a cosmic conflict between Christ and Satan, Good and Evil, Truth and Error. Reduced to its most basic essentials, it's a battle for our **hearts** and **minds**. You and I are not *passive spectators* merely watching from the sidelines—we're deeply involved as *key participants*, whether we like it or not, and whether we even realize it or not!

This war against God BEGAN in Heaven with Lucifer's rebellion—but it's going to END on this earth with God's victory and vindication. It's the most UNCIVIL war in history, and it's "a fight to the finish" that is DEADLY—remember how the devil or "Dragon" tried to kill Jesus from the moment He was born? (See Revelation 12:1–5 and Matthew 2:1–23.) Fortunately, this colossal conflict is—in God's divine plan—the war to END all wars.

But for *now*, the battle is raging right here on Planet Earth, a war zone which has become "the Theater of the Universe." The apostle Paul says in **1 Corinthians 4:9** that "We have been made a **spectacle** to the **world**, both to angels and to men." The Greek word Paul wrote for "spectacle" is *theatron*, from which we get our English word "theater." And the Greek word translated "world" is *kosmos*, from which we derive our words "cosmos" and "universe."

Just as some TV addicts are hooked on soap operas to see what "Dick" and "Jane" will do in their latest crisis, the whole UNIVERSE is watching US—with intense interest—to see what *we* will do, whose side *we* will choose, in the great controversy between Christ and Satan! No trivial soap opera with its *fictional* characters could be half as interesting as the real thing, on which hang eternal destinies.

Even Shakespeare's line that *"All the world's a stage"* pales into insignificance compared to the awesome stakes involved here. For this controversy has all the aspects of a melodramatic play and is, in fact, the DRAMA OF THE AGES! Satan is the villain; Christ is the hero. There's a tragic plot—with intrigue and conflict—and a magnificent cast of characters involving not only kings and popes but even you and me! We may wear different costumes and act out different roles, but we each have a part, a vital part to play in this drama.

So Paul brings in the image of a drama—one that's better than any "Reality TV." But let's not forget that *we're not just actors in a "play"* but *soldiers* in a *battle* involving life and death.

All of us humans are inducted into this titanic battle the day we're born. So there's NO DISCHARGE in this war. No one can simply say, "Wake me when it's over." And when we become Christians we stand a good chance of becoming special targets of Satan. But I have *good* news, GREAT news for you: Now listen . . . *confidentially, I read the back of the Book*—and WE WIN!!!

It's very good to know that those who follow God are on the winning side. But since the battle's still raging, we *still* face a supernatural enemy who *hates* us and wants to *deceive* us so he can take US down *with* him.

Let's kindly remember that those who have become involved in Contemplative Prayer are not bad, they're not evil, they're believers like us. Even religious leaders who are quite sincere may at times be misled. They themselves could be honestly deceived. They simply feel that Contemplative Prayer seems right. But . . . just because it **SEEMS right** doesn't mean it **IS right**—as we'll try to show those people in this study—and everyone else who cares about what the Bible says regarding these things.

So let's begin by looking at some pertinent Bible verses for background.

- **Revelation 12:7–9, 12** — *"War broke out in HEAVEN [!]:* Michael and his angels fought with the **dragon;** and the dragon and his angels fought, but they did not prevail, nor was a place found for them in heaven any longer. So the great dragon was cast out, that **serpent** of old, called the **Devil** and **Satan,** who deceives the **whole world**; he was cast to the earth, and his angels were cast out with him. . . . **Woe** to the inhabitants of the earth! . . . For *the Devil has come down to you, having great wrath, because he knows that he has [but] a short time."*

- **1 Peter 5:8** — "Be sober, be vigilant; because **your adversary the Devil** walks about *like a roaring LION,* seeking whom he may **DEVOUR.**"

- **2 Corinthians 2:11** — We must be alert and beware, "lest Satan should take advantage of us; for *we are not ignorant of his devices.*"

- **2 Corinthians 11:13–15** — The apostle Paul warns us against those who "are *false* apostles, *deceitful* workers, *transforming themselves into apostles of Christ.* **And no wonder! For Satan himself transforms himself into an ANGEL of light.** Therefore *it is no great thing* if his **MINISTERS** also transform themselves into *ministers of righteousness,* whose **END** will be according to their works."

- **1 Timothy 4:1, KJV** — "Now the Spirit speaketh expressly, that *in the latter times* some shall *depart from the faith,* giving heed to *seducing spirits, and doctrines of devils."*

- **1 John 4:1** — "Beloved, *do not believe every spirit,* but *TEST* the spirits, whether they are of God; because many false prophets have gone out into the world."

My hope and prayer is that you'll take those Bible passages as seriously as God intended, for *these pages you're reading are not at all a routine report of everyday facts.* Instead, they must be an urgent wake-up call, a red flag, a solemn warning—in short, a cry of alarm to everyone I can reach.

The cause of my great concern is that I've recently learned of a diabolical strategy that—in all seriousness—threatens the very survival of Christianity, at least as we know it. The devil, reading the prophetic signs of the times better than anyone else, knows he has but a short time, for Christ will soon return. Therefore, in these last days "Satan's pulling out all the stops" and attacking *ALL* the churches with *this "granddaddy" of all heresies!*

Some of those who are completely devoted to the New Age movement are so deceived by Satan that they unwittingly consent to have themselves—their bodies, minds, and voices—used as "channels" for *spirit entities who are actually demons* posing as mystic "masters" who supposedly lived centuries ago. A few of those "gifted psychics" even achieve popular celebrity status. No doubt scattered over the world are many more of those mediumistic channelers who contact and invite into their minds the *purported* "dead departed" (who are really clever devils) and converse with them. But even so, such mystics still were relatively few in number—until recently.

For in just the last few decades, *ancient Eastern mysticism* has been revived and is infiltrating almost ALL Christian churches in the Western world. It's as if one of Satan's demons suggested to his Infernal Highness:

> We've had good success with those celebrity channelers of the New Age—but they're still a mere handful. Just think what our legions could do if we *popularized mysticism* among church-goers everywhere *so that ALL Christians allow us to speak to them each time they PRAY!*

Satan saw that the evil results of this proposal could be—and would be—horrendously *delightful* from his point of view. And "the rest," as they say, "is history"—the history and heresy of **Contemplative Prayer.**

This study has **THREE parts. First,** we'll see what Contemplative Prayer *IS* and *HOW* it works. **Second,** we'll examine its *roots* and *sources* to learn *WHERE* it comes from. **Third,** we'll consider its *deadly DANGERS*—the *perils* of Contemplative Prayer to everyone seduced into its practice.

So let's take a good, hard look at this hazardous heresy. To understand its all-out assault on Christianity, let's *dissect* the *anatomy* of this *whole subject*—its sources, its promoters and proponents, and its dangers.

As a quick preview, let me simply **LIST some relevant TERMS** you'll encounter. *I'll define and explain these terms below as we proceed,* but for now just take a quick look at some seemingly harmless code-words used by those devoted to this heresy:

> Spiritual Formation ● Contemplative Prayer ● Centering Prayer ● "The Silence"
> ● Mantra ● Meditation ● The Emerging or Emergent Church ● Universalism ●
> Monism ● Pantheism ● Panentheism ● Zen Buddhism ● Mystical Experiences
> ● Spiritual Directors ● Spiritual Disciplines

The first term is . . .

Spiritual Formation = An all-inclusive term that covers everything discussed in this study. In fact, I could have used this broad, "umbrella" term in my *title,* but I choose instead to refer specifically to Contemplative Prayer because that mystical practice—with its resultant "Silence" and exposure to demonic influence—is the crux of this deadly problem and the focus of this study.

Spiritual Formation is a system of practices invented in 1548 by Ignatius Loyola, the Roman Catholic founder of the Jesuits, to train the young Jesuit priest to submit his mind and will to his superiors.[1] The one who trains him has the title of **Spiritual Director.**

So it is that even today, someone who is *not* a Jesuit, and *not* a priest, and *not even a member* of the Roman Catholic Church, but who is nevertheless *willing* to submit to Spiritual Formation and learn its practices, will have a human Spiritual Director appointed to guide him or her.[2]

The Spiritual Director is of course *trained* to do this sort of thing, but the fact remains that the new situation puts *a human being in charge* of personally directing the student, and all too often *this trusted person takes the place of the Bible* in the student's intimate spiritual life.

Contemplative Prayer, *also called* **Centering Prayer,** is a method of prayer that is supposed to lead a person into contemplation. It is supposed to be done for twenty minutes in the morning and twenty minutes in the evening. The person chooses a "sacred word"—a "mantra"—and tries to *ignore all thoughts and feelings,* letting them go by as boats going down a stream. When the thoughts keep coming back and interfering, the person returns to repeating the sacred word. The goal is to keep practicing until ALL THOUGHTS AND FEELINGS DISAPPEAR.

Roman Catholic Abbot [3] Thomas Keating says in *Open Mind, Open Heart,* "All thoughts pass if you wait long enough." [4] A person then reaches a state of pure consciousness or a *mental void* known as "the Silence." *The thinking process is suspended.* This technique is supposed to put them into direct contact with God. The idea is to go to "the center" of your being to find your "True Self." This process is supposed to dismantle the "False Self," which is supposedly the result of the emotional baggage we carry.

Contemplative Prayer is thus a ***mystical*** prayer practice that leads one into "the Silence" but in actuality leads away from God. The word *mystical* means the attempt of mystics to use *occult*—that is, *hidden* or *secret*—methods and techniques to make ***direct*** contact with their god or gods. The *Hindu swami* or *yogi,* the *African medicine man* or *witch doctor* are all *mystic masters* who go into a trance to commune with spirit entities who supposedly give them secret KNOWLEDGE or POWER. While in the silence of their trancelike state, this knowledge or power comes to them ***directly*** from the spirit world of demons—*NOT* from the study of any scriptures.

So contemplative spirituality is a belief system that uses *ancient mystical practices* to induce an *altered state of consciousness* ("the Silence"). Contemplative spirituality is often attractively wrapped in *Christian* terminology, but the theological premise is the *pagan* worldview of **pantheism** (**ALL** is God) and/or **panentheism** (God is **IN all**).

The purpose of Contemplative Prayer is to enter an "altered state of consciousness" in order to find one's "true self"—thus finding **God!** This true self relates to the belief that man is basically good. Promoters of Contemplative Prayer teach that ALL human beings (religious *and* non-religious) have a ***DIVINE*** center and that ALL—not just born-again believers—should practice Contemplative Prayer.

A. Mantras, Meditation, and Mysticism

Some of you who have studied Hinduism know that Hindu mystics use a "mantra" while meditating. A **mantra** is a sacred syllable, word, or phrase (usually in Sanskrit, the ancient language of Hinduism) *chanted repeatedly* to aid in focusing the mind in meditation. In Contemplative or Centering Prayer, people are taught to choose and repeat a special word to *empty their minds.* The Catholic mystic Thomas Keating doesn't like to call it a "mantra"—that's why proponents call it, instead, attractive, innocent-sounding terms like a "prayer word" or "sacred word" which don't come from the Sanskrit language or Eastern pagan religions.

But if it's used to rid the mind of all thoughts and feelings, *it does the same thing as a mantra.* And as Shakespeare said, "A rose by *any other name* would smell as sweet." [5] Christian author Ray Yungen, in his excellent book *A Time of Departing,* explains:

> Since *mantras* are central to New Age meditation, it is important to understand a proper definition of the word. The translation from Sanskrit is *man,* meaning "to think," and *tra,* meaning "to be liberated from." [6] Thus, the word literally means *to escape from thought.* By repeating the mantra, either out loud or silently, the word or phrase begins to *lose* any meaning it once had. The conscious thinking process is gradually *tuned out* until *an altered state of consciousness* is achieved. [7]

John Main (1926–1982) was a Benedictine monk who popularized a Contemplative Prayer form known appropriately as *"the way of the mantra,"* which was first taught to him by a Hindu monk. [8] Richard Foster, in his book *Spiritual Classics,* says Main "rediscovered meditation" from the "Far East." [9] Main explains his "way of the mantra" as follows:

> Listen to the mantra as you say it, gently but continuously [*that is, repeatedly*]. . . . If thoughts or images come, these are distractions at the time of meditation, so return simply to saying your word. Simply ignore it [the distraction], and the way to ignore it is to say your mantra. Return with fidelity to meditation each morning and evening for between twenty and thirty minutes. [10]

The mystic goal is to reach a *mental void* of "pure consciousness" in order to find God at the center. This is *exactly* what Hindus and Buddhists have done for thousands of years to reach god-consciousness or pure consciousness. This is also similar to what New Age actress Shirley MacLaine does to go into an altered level of consciousness and discover her "Divine Center" or "Higher Self," which is her supposed *divinity.*

The Cloud of Unknowing, an early book on Contemplative Prayer—one of the most well known on the subject—was written about 1375 by an anonymous Catholic monk who teaches:

> Take just a little word, of one syllable rather than of two. . . . With this word you are to **strike down every kind of thought** under the cloud of forgetting. [11]

Willigis Jager, a Catholic Benedictine monk and master of Zen Buddhism, adds this instruction to our use of the mantra:

> Do *NOT* reflect on the **meaning** of the word; **thinking and reflecting must CEASE,** as all mystical writers insist. Simply "sound" the word silently, letting go of ALL feelings and thoughts. [12]

The testimony is uniform on the use of mantras or "sacred words." Let me add a statement here by Catholic priest Henri Nouwen (1932–1996), a popular author and professor who, following the ancient Hindu masters, taught the repeating of a **mantra** as we approach God in prayer:

> *The quiet* **REPETITION** *of a single word* can help us *to descend with the* mind *into the* heart. . . . This way of simple prayer . . . opens us to God's active **presence**. [13]

B. Talk About *Repetition!!!*

I'm not sure readers can grasp the full import of what we've said so far in this study, but I want to tell you that when Contemplative Prayer teachers say "repetition" they *MEAN repetition!* For example, J. P. Moreland and Klaus Issler are both professors at Talbot School of Theology at Biola University and co-authors of *The Lost Virtue of Happiness* in which they make the following recommendations, among others:

> We recommend that you **begin** by saying the Jesus Prayer about **three hundred times a day**. . . . **When you first awaken, say the Jesus Prayer twenty to thirty times**. . . . **Repetitive use of the Jesus Prayer while doing more focused things** allows God to be on the boundaries of your mind. . . . [14]

In regard to repetition, Christian author Roger Oakland shares this experience:

> I have been to the country of Myanmar (formerly called Burma) twice. On both occasions, I observed and videotaped both Catholics and Buddhists practicing **repetitive** *prayer.* By the way, in both cases they were chanting these prayers OVER and OVER again while counting *BEADS.* Yes, *Catholics and Buddhists both have a ROSARY technique* to keep track of how many times they have chanted a prayer. [15]

Oakland adds that he also *interviewed* Catholics and Buddhists praying in Myanmar, asking what they were doing and why. Each time he asked, he was told the same thing: It's a way to *focus their thoughts* and *get in tune with **the spirit world***. Oakland concludes that chanting repetitive phrases to get closer to God is NOT biblical—it's satanic. While **called** Christian, these doctrines of so-called ancient wisdom are **anything but** Christian!

The many books out there teaching Contemplative Prayer all sing the praises of repeating the mantra and emphasizing its importance. But *IS there*, after all, a **RIGHT** way and **WRONG** way to pray? Jesus may have been calling our attention to a *wrong* way as He said: *"But when you pray, do NOT use vain REPETITIONS as the heathen do."* —**Matthew 6:7.**

So with the Master's words in mind as a stern warning, I don't think Heaven's plan is for us Christians to babble a mantra, thoughtlessly reciting it, repeating it—as the Eastern religions do—until they "go out of their mind" and into "the Silence."

C. DECEPTIVELY SWITCHING LABELS

A major part of the strategy by Centering Prayer's proponents is to confuse Christian seekers through **a confusion of TERMS**—quite *innocent-sounding* terms (for instance, "sacred word" for *mantra*, or "the Silence" for *trance)*—so that no one will realize, or even suspect, that he or she is being deceived. Contemplative Prayer has always been the historic name for this practice; then around 1978 the Catholic monks Thomas Keating and Basil Pennington started calling it Centering Prayer; now just a year or two ago the term "Listening Prayer" seems to be the new label which may catch on.

What we're dealing with is really <u>ancient sorcery</u> *dressed up* in <u>Christian terminology</u>. For example, take the basic word <u>prayer</u>. *Who can find fault with prayer?* Believers of all faiths pray to their deity or deities—asking advice, seeking help, offering praise and thanks. But as we shall see, Christians must realize that Contemplative Prayer is *neither* "Christian" *nor* "prayer."

Or take the word <u>meditation</u>. In the Western world, *meditation* means to *think* deeply about *something, turning it over slowly and carefully in your mind.* But in the pagan East—the mystical East of Hinduism and Buddhism—it means to *EMPTY the mind* in order *to open it to the SPIRIT world,* leading to *mystical* experiences—supposedly even with "God" Himself!

The same deceptive ploy is used with many other marketing terms to make this movement more attractive, terms like *contemplation, emerging, vintage,* and *spiritual*—all those words seem pleasant and positive, but you get the idea. This technique of "switching labels" is cunningly designed to "lead us down the primrose path" to deception without our catching on.

But Centering Prayer, a foundational contemplative technique, is nothing more—or less—than a "Christianized" version of *Eastern mystical meditation.* Stripped of its deceptively <u>biblical</u>-sounding terminology, it's <u>no different</u> from that which Hindu yogis have practiced for *millennia*—and neither are its spiritual *dangers,* as we shall see.

Most Contemplative Prayer teachers announce that such prayer is *NOT* a "technique"—and then they go on to recommend *various* techniques. For example, in his book *Prayer: Finding the Heart's True Home,* Richard Foster recommends the practice of Breath Prayer [16]—picking a single word or short phrase and repeating it in conjunction with breath rhythms. Ray Yungen says, "This is classic contemplative *mysticism,*" and then adds:

> I once related Foster's Breath Prayer method to a former New Age devotee who is now a Christian. She affirmed this [mystical] connection when she remarked with astonishment, *"That's what I did when I was into* ashtanga *yoga!"* [17]

Tricia Rhodes, a favorite author of Pastor Rick Warren, also gives instructions on a slight variation of Breath Prayer:

> Take deep breaths, concentrating on relaxing your body. Establish a slow, rhythmic pattern. Breathe in God's peace, and breathe out your stresses, distractions, and fears. *Breathe in God's love,* forgiveness, and compassion, *and breathe out your sins,* failures, and frustrations. Make every effort to stop the flow of talking going on within you—to slow it down until it comes to a halt. [18]

Do you recall ever reading in Scripture that you could partake of **God's LOVE** by physically *breathing it IN* or could **rid yourself of SIN** by *breathing it OUT?* All these New Age mystics and compromising Christians who put on airs of brilliance and "the higher wisdom of the ancient masters" are aptly described by God in **Romans 1:22,** KJV — "Professing themselves to be wise, they became fools."

But the reality is that when dangerous or evil things are *misnamed* with "good" labels, honest-seekers-after-truth may at first become intrigued and interested, then slightly confused, and finally they let down their guard enough to gladly go "like lambs to the slaughter."

D. "THE SILENCE"

Center stage in the Contemplative Prayer drama is "<u>the Silence</u>." For basic to the teaching of Contemplative Prayer are the unbiblical and misleading notions that "*true*" prayer is: *silent, beyond words, beyond thought.*

What "the Silence" is really like is described quite clearly by William Johnston, who is not only a *Jesuit priest* but also a *Zen Buddhist* master:

When one enters the deeper layers of Contemplative Prayer one sooner or later experiences the *void*, the *emptiness,* the *nothingness* . . . the profound mystical SILENCE . . . an ABSENCE of thought. [19]

Jesuit priest and mystic teacher Anthony de Mello adds this:

To silence the mind is an *extremely difficult task. How hard it is* to keep the mind from thinking, thinking, thinking, forever thinking, forever producing thoughts in a never-ending stream. *Our Hindu masters in India* have a saying: "one thorn is removed by another." By this they mean that you will be wise to *use one thought to rid yourself of all the other thoughts* that crowd into your mind. One thought, one image, one phrase or sentence or word [your *mantra*] that your mind can be made to fasten on. [20]

Richard Foster, perhaps the most successful promoter of Contemplative Prayer, writes of how *essential* "the Silence" is in these words:

Contemplative Prayer immerses us into the silence of God. How desperately we in the modern world **NEED** *this wordless baptism! . . . Progress in intimacy with God means progress toward **silence.*** [21] . . . **EVERY** distraction of the body, mind, and spirit **MUST** be put into a kind of ***suspended animation*** **BEFORE** this deep work of God upon the soul can occur. [22]

But students of God's Word, the Bible, know that "Silence is [*not always*] Golden"!

The original "centering prayer" book[23] by Basil Pennington, a Trappist monk, is really a rehash of Eastern spirituality. The technique is still one where you put the intellect on "hold." You are urged to *dismiss* all thoughts, *hold on to* no thoughts, *react to* no thoughts, *retain* no thoughts. Those are some of Pennington's phrases. And *why?* The rational mind is one of the God-given gifts of what it means to be a human being. And we never find Christ saying: "Stop thinking. Stop using reason. Clear your mind." He never taught that.

Catholic monk and abbot Thomas Keating, one of the foremost teachers of Centering Prayer, says in his book *Open Mind, Open Heart,*

As you go down deeper, you may reach a place where the sacred word disappears altogether and there are *NO thoughts.* This is often experienced as a *suspension of CONSCIOUSNESS,* a space. [24]

This "suspension of consciousness" Keating calls "a space." Most people would call it "a trance" and do call it that—which brings us to the next point in our discussion.

E. TRANCES AND HYPNOTISM, ANYONE?

Roman Catholic priest John D. Dreher has studied Centering Prayer in depth for years and has sounded many warnings of its dangers. His careful assessment leads him to this conclusion:

> Centering Prayer is essentially a form of self-hypnosis. It makes use of a "mantra," a word repeated over and over to focus the mind while striving by one's will to go deep within oneself. The effects are a hypnotic-like state: *concentration upon one thing, disengagement from other stimuli, a high degree of openness to suggestion, a psychological and physiological condition that externally resembles sleep but in which consciousness is interiorized and the mind subject to suggestion.*
>
> After reading a published description of centering prayer, a psychology professor said, "Your question is, Is this hypnosis? Sure it is." He said the [hypnotic] state can be verified physiologically by *the drop in blood pressure, respiratory rate, lactic acid level in the blood, and the galvanic conductivity of the skin.* Abbot Keating relates that, when they began doing the Centering Prayer workshops in the guest house, some of the monks and guests "complained that it was *spooky* seeing people walking around the guest house like 'zombies.' " They recognized the symptoms but could not diagnose the illness. [25]

New Age therapist Jacquelyn Small quite plainly agrees with the hypnotic effect of "the Silence"—though she is guilty of falsely calling Contemplative Prayer "Christian" when she describes it:

> A form of *Christian* meditation, its practitioners are trained to focus on an inner symbol [a mantra] *that QUIETS the MIND. . . .* When practitioners become skilled at this method of meditation, they undergo *a DEEP TRANCE state similar to AUTO-HYPNOSIS.* [26]

Marcia Montenegro, before turning to Christ and becoming a Christian activist against occult deceptions, was deeply involved in many aspects of New Age mystical beliefs and practices. She was also a professional astrologer for eight years, and the inside information gained during her former wide experience as a deeply involved New Ager enables her to shine a bright light on the dark side of today's so-called spirituality. Her book *Spellbound: The Paranormal Seduction of Today's Kids* was published in 2006. And she says this about trances:

> The *trance* or *meditative state* is BASIC to the work of witches, psychics, sorcerers, ritual magicians, channelers [spirit mediums of the "dead"], and is used in past-life regressions. *It is the SAME state of mind reached with meditation techniques taught today.* Some cultures/ groups use *drugs [hallucinogenic drugs]* to reach this state. [27]

She also tells us that "the late Sybil Leek, a well-known witch and psychic, while concentrating on a crystal during a reading, induces a trance *both* in the <u>client</u> *and* in the <u>psychic</u> in order to release 'dormant psychic awareness.'" [28]

The August 2010 cover story of the influential magazine *Christianity Today* featured **Beth Moore**, whom the article calls *"the most popular Bible teacher in America."* Moore is also a strong proponent of Contemplative Prayer and, incidentally, she is noted in *Christianity Today* for influencing "millions" of women through her organization *Living Proof Ministries*.

Beth Moore participated (along with authors Richard Foster and Max Lucado) as a narrator for a 2006 *Fox Home Entertainment* film titled *Be Still*—a DVD "infomercial" for contemplative spirituality. The DVD's purpose is not to instruct in Contemplative Prayer but rather *to make you and your family hungry for it.* And if Moore has the potential of leading "millions" of women, as *Christianity Today* reports, this DVD could steer them in a spiritually dangerous direction. *Those women in turn will bring this mystical teaching home to their husbands, children, and churches.*

In the *Be Still* DVD, Beth Moore emphatically states:

> [I]f we are **not STILL** before Him [God], we *will* **<u>NEVER</u>** *truly know to the depths of the marrow of our bones that He is God.* **There's <u>GOT</u> to be a STILLNESS.** [29]

Moore says that it is **not possible** to "truly know" that He is God without "a stillness." She's not talking about a quiet place to pray and spend time in God's Word, but *rather she's talking about a stillness of the MIND*—this is what contemplatives strive for. Unless you practice this stillness of the mind, your relationship with the Lord is inadequate. According to Beth Moore, you don't even know Him in the way you should.

In her 2002 book, *When Godly People Do Ungodly Things,* Moore gives a clue as to how devoted she is to a life of Contemplative Prayer. She states:

> I have picked up on the terminology of Brother Lawrence [*a mystic Carmelite monk who said* **he "cried out, singing and dancing violently like a madman"** *when he went into the "presence"* [30]], who called praying unceasingly practicing God's presence. In fact, practicing God's presence has been my number-one goal for the last year. [31]

Mystic Brennan Manning, a former Catholic priest, has become quite respected in contemplative circles—his followers include popular Christians such as authors Max Lucado and Philip Yancey, and musical artists Michael Card and Amy Grant. But he leads them into "the Silence" of Contemplative Prayer by teaching the following **three instructions:**

"The *first step in faith* is to **STOP THINKING ABOUT GOD at the time of prayer.**" [32] But the time of prayer is *when it's most natural to think about God!*

"Choose a single, sacred word [to use as a mantra] . . . *REPEAT* the sacred word inwardly, slowly, and *OFTEN*." [33]

"Enter into the great silence of God. Alone in that silence, the noise within will subside and the Voice of Love will be heard." [34] *Capital letters in Manning's original imply Deity.*

If we let them, some people will *MAKE UP religion as they go along.* But, again, the vital question for Bible believers to ask is: **Did Jesus** instruct His followers to *empty their minds* through Contemplative Prayer? On the contrary, in **Matthew 22:37** He said: "You shall love the Lord your God with all your heart, with all your soul, and with **ALL** your **MIND**."

All this dogmatic praise of "the Silence" leads one to think that God's Word, the Bible, is *little more than a philosophy and needs the help of Contemplative Prayer to be effective at all.* The insinuation is also that *the Holy Spirit is dormant and ineffective without this "vital" stimuli.* But Jesus Himself said in **Matthew 6:6** that the only "stillness" necessary for prayer is the kind you find in your room with the door shut:

> "But you, when you pray, go into your room, and when you have shut your door, pray to your Father who is in the secret place; and your Father who sees in secret will reward you openly."

F. "Clutching at Straws" in the Scriptures

Reasonably enough, we expect Christian clergy to teach Christian doctrine. We want to see what Bible backing they may have for what they claim, what Scriptural support there is for what they teach. We know that any good, valid doctrine always has a *"Thus saith the Lord"* behind it, so we expect Christian teachers to point to a specific chapter and verse in the Bible that *explicitly validates* what they claim.

But since the Bible *does not teach* Contemplative Prayer, its promoters find it hard to support it—at least among Christians who care about such things. So they try to use Scripture texts that *SEEM* somewhat helpful to their cause *though they are NOT*—even if such a practice is unethical.

Scripture Text #1: Psalm 46:10

One such example is that *the very title* of the *Be Still* video is taken completely out of context. The lone line quoted on the video cover reads: *"Be still, and know that I am God"*—from **Psalm 46:10.** But the larger context shows that <u>this psalm is not speaking of PRAYER at all</u>! Let's analyze it to learn the truth.

The psalm begins with a divine promise: *"God is our refuge and strength, a very present help in trouble. Therefore we will not fear."* It mentions *"the city of God, the holy place of the tabernacle of the Most High,"* which may be attacked and besieged by enemy armies, but *"God is in the midst of her, she shall not be moved; God shall help her."* And when military action came, note God's response: *"The nations raged, the kingdoms were moved; <u>He uttered His voice, the earth **MELTED**</u>."* Centuries later, on stormy Galilee, Jesus majestically calmed the threatening tempest with no other instrument than His voice. [35] How ***mighty*** is a word from God!

Then we're invited to behold with fixed attention the *"desolations"* made by God's delivering power, as if these are still visible. Broken bows, splintered spears, charred chariots strew the ground, and Israel could go forth without fear and feast their eyes on these tokens of what God had done for them. *"Come, behold the **works** of the Lord, who has made **desolations** in the earth. He makes wars cease to the end of the earth; He **breaks** the bow and **cuts** the spear in two; He **burns** the chariot in the fire."*

Against this picture of history's **battlefield**, littered with broken, abandoned weapons once held in hands now turned to dust, we come upon **the very next verse:** *"Be still, and know that I am God."*

The Hebrew word translated "be still" is *raphah*. Scholars tell us that in its true context it literally means "stay put" or "desist" or "don't move hastily." God desires that His foes would stop fighting against Him before it proves fatal to them. Renowned Bible scholar Matthew Henry tells us:

> So God says to His enemies, *"Cease* your vain strife. *Stand still,* and threaten no more. But **know**—to your terror—that I am God, the Almighty One, who is infinitely above you and too strong for you." And He says to His own people, *"Be calm* and tremble no more, but **know**—to your comfort—that the Lord of hosts is with you; the God of Jacob is your refuge." [36]

Spokesmen for the *Be Still* video may try to argue, "Well, we don't agree with those ideas, for this is simply a matter of one's *interpretation!*" But that's **not true** at all. It's much more a matter of <u>linguistic correctness</u>—and perhaps a pinch of integrity of character. Evidence of that is the fact that ***several modern Bible versions*** bear out the "interpretation" presented here: that in this verse of **Psalm 46:10** *God wisely warns the enemies who strive against Him* to **"Cease** and **desist!"** Please note such examples as these:

● *New American Standard Bible* — **"Cease striving** and know that I am God."

- *Good News Translation* — " 'Stop fighting,' He says, 'and know that I am God.' "
- *Holman Christian Standard* — "Stop your fighting—and know that I am God."
- *Complete Jewish Bible* — "Desist, and learn that I am God."
- *Young's Literal Translation* — "Desist, and know that I am God."

We all know that in English, the ordinary phrase "Be still" could be a command for either *vocal* stillness (as in "Don't say a word!") or *physical* stillness (as in "Don't move a muscle!"), and the Hebrew *raphah* denotes the LATTER. But . . . mystic teachers of Contemplative Prayer reject BOTH of those possibilities and want it to mean a THIRD type, a *mental* stillness in a *mind emptied of every thought and feeling!* Unfortunately for them, the verse they try to use does <u>*NOT* in any way</u> suggest an exercise for emptying the mind for silent prayer. Period! [37]

SCRIPTURE TEXT #2: MATTHEW 6:6

Here we find another Bible verse *misused* and *abused* by someone who should know better. Thomas Keating, a Trappist monk and Catholic mystic, is recognized as one of the founders of the modern Contemplative/Centering Prayer movement. And he travels at times, tirelessly conducting well-attended *seminars* and *retreats* teaching and promoting Centering Prayer—*in 1991 alone, he taught thirty-one thousand people how to "listen to God"!* [38]

One of the people who attended one of his "LECTURES AND MEDITATIVE SESSIONS" was Marcia Montenegro. Ms. Montenegro has *a very interesting background,* because she was formerly a professional astrologer who practiced *Hindu, Tibetan Buddhist, Zen Buddhist,* and *New Age* **meditation** for many years before God led her to salvation in Christ in December 1990, and has since become quite knowledgeable in the Bible.

She and a friend attended Keating's lecture having the deliberate intention of listening intently, taking careful notes, and seeing exactly what he was teaching in a live situation. I am indebted to her insightful account, which I share as follows with thanks: [39]

> Keating came forward and gave instructions on how to do Centering Prayer (he called it Centering Prayer though it's also known as Contemplative Prayer). He claimed that ***"Silence is God's first language,"*** but Montenegro said she knows of *no evidence* for this—*and none was given.* Language comes from God: We humans communicate and speak in words because that is how God made us, as one of the big distinctions between us and the animal world. **Genesis 1:3** tells us "God said, '**Let there be light**'; and there was light." So, according to the Bible, God spoke even *before* He created man.

Keating said that Centering Prayer is a "description of *Jesus' formula* for interior silence"—though Keating admitted that *Jesus did not give much detail on this.* [Comment by Montenegro: "Jesus gave **NO** details on it!"]

A lengthy teaching now began on the single verse of **Matthew 6:6**, where Jesus tells people to go into the "inner room" (NASB—or just "room" in most other versions; KJV says "closet") and "shut the door and pray to your Father who is in secret. And your Father who sees in secret will reward you" (quoting **Matthew 6:6**).

Keating claimed that *THIS is the "formula" Jesus gave us for Centering Prayer!* The "inner room" is "our inner self" where we are to retreat or enter through Centering Prayer. Then we "shut the door," letting go of our "ordinary psychological awareness" and perceptions.

Yet a simple reading of the *preceding* verse shows that **Matthew 6:6** is *a strong <u>contrast</u> to the picture of "the hypocrites" in verse 5 who pray PUBLICLY to get attention.* Jesus is saying, in essence, "*Don't show off* when you pray; don't be like the hypocrites who make a big deal of praying just to look good." Jesus was <u>NOT</u> talking at all about so-called "*interior silence*" and "*withdrawing into one's self*" when He said we should go to the inner room! The inner room was a small room in houses where people could go for PRIVATE prayer. [40] Jesus, the Master Teacher, is speaking quite plainly and being *literal* here—not masking His meaning in hidden metaphors.

SCRIPTURE TEXT #3: 1 KINGS 19:12

A third Bible verse is sometimes tried to be put to service—but fails to support the teaching of Contemplative Prayer. People sometimes ask if **1 Kings 19:12** is an example of when Contemplative Prayer is condoned in Scripture. The prophet Elijah heard "*a still small voice.*" Isn't that referring to "the Silence"? Author Ray Yungen wisely observes that this passage in no way indicates that Elijah was practicing mantra meditation.

On the contrary, it was the *pagan* priests of Baal (a heathen nature god) who REPEATEDLY "called on the name of Baal from *morning* till *noon,* and then even till the time of the *evening* sacrifice, saying, 'O Baal, hear us!' " — **1 Kings 18:26** — but read the whole passage of **1 Kings 18:17–40**. *It's one of God's most thrilling victories in all the Bible!*

Now Elijah was in a cave (see **1 Kings 19:9–18**), not to practice Contemplative Prayer, but to hide from Jezebel's threat to take his life. Also, his encounter with God was something *HE did not initiate* but God Himself initiated—thereby emphasizing that Elijah was **NOT** practicing a mantra.

And he and the Lord had *a regular conversation* at some length, each one **speaking** and responding with normal _vocalized words_—not with _mere thoughts_ in "the Silence." A simple reading of **1 Kings 19:9–18** shows that this audible conversation occurred both **before** and **after** the "still small voice" was heard in verse **12!** Yungen says, "If anything, from his conversation with God, we might conclude that he was hiding from his ministry and from God Himself, as he was feeling hopeless."

Most theologians read **1 Kings 19:11–12** as an object lesson to Elijah on the nature of the great God. The majestic Lord of heaven and earth chose _NOT_ to reveal Himself in the mighty power of the awesome windstorm, the convulsive earthquake, or the flaming fire. Instead, God spoke to the prophet by "a still small voice." So Jesus, meek and mild—but almighty—was to do His work, _NOT_ with the clash of arms and the overturning of thrones and kingdoms, but through speaking to the hearts of men by a life of service and self-sacrifice.

G. Is Contemplative Prayer _REALLY_ an Advanced Form of Christian Prayer?

Advocates for Contemplative Prayer make their brainchild sound so special, as if it's a wonderful, "advanced form of Christian prayer," that the unsuspecting public is often sold on it. But before they "buy" the lies peddled in today's marketplace of ideas, they need to wake up to the fact that it's _NOT so special,_ and _NOT so advanced._ In fact, upon investigation, Contemplative Prayer proves itself to be _NOT Christian_ at all—and _NOT prayer_ at all! Let's keep this simple by considering each of these two aspects separately.

1. Is Contemplative Prayer _CHRISTIAN?_

First, to answer the question "Is Contemplative Prayer _Christian?_" we must address the _broader_ issue: **What makes ANY teaching Christian?** The answer could be stated affirmatively in at least three ways: A teaching is a Christian teaching **(1)** if **Jesus** taught it, or **(2)** if **His apostles** taught it, or **(3)** if it is supported by the black ink of **the New Testament**.

In other words, any teaching must be considered truly Christian if its teachers can _point to specific chapters and verses in the Bible_ showing that it meets at least _ONE_ of those three criteria. The teachers of Contemplative Prayer DO NOT do that because they CANNOT do that—for the simple reason that _IT DID NOT COME FROM THE BIBLE, God's Holy Word!_

On the other hand, we who oppose these mystical teachings and try to protect the church against them, easily display **a wealth of evidence** showing that *mystical mantras with their meditative trances of spirit-filled "silence" have their roots and sources in the ancient non-Christian religions of Hinduism and Buddhism.*

And furthermore, those mystic practices—which God ***forbids!***—infiltrated the Christian church *much later* through the avenue of Roman Catholicism, whose monks and mystics handed it on to Protestant leaders who were at first few in number but who nevertheless succeeded in widely popularizing it.

Those who persist in calling *mystic meditation* "Christian" are severely damaging their own credibility. The simplest way to prove them wrong is to note the apostles' request, ***"Lord, teach us to pray"*** in **Luke 11:1.** They sincerely wanted to know the right way to pray. And in His reply, Jesus, the Master Teacher, did not so much as to **HINT** that they needed to "empty their minds" *in order to practice Contemplative Prayer!*

Thus the **EVIDENCE** that anyone must use in answering this question is *very much AGAINST* calling Contemplative Prayer "Christian" and *very much in FAVOR of* recognizing it unequivocally as a pagan intruder from ancient Eastern religions, as we shall see below.

2. Is Contemplative Prayer *EVEN PRAYER?*

Most people have a rather good idea what traditional, biblical prayer is like, but let's look at a few Scriptural facts of this type of prayer just to refresh our minds.

From many examples in the Bible, we learn that **prayer uses WORDS** to express our thoughts and feelings, our desires, hopes and dreams, our ambitions and disappointments to God. In prayer we can praise God, expressing our love and adoration for Him. We can seek His divine help and guidance. But God *expects* us to ASK: **James 4:2,** KJV, says: "Ye *HAVE not* because ye *ASK not."* **And** Jesus recommends in **John 16:23** that we ask *in His name* when we pray.

While I believe prayer should *always be respectful and reverent,* befitting our address to the Supreme Being, I also believe one can view God as a *loving heavenly Father,* as Jesus taught us in the Lord's Prayer, so *we can talk to Him as an intimate Friend.*

But the Bible is clear, the prayers of unbelievers are not heard by God: "Now we know that God does not hear sinners; but if anyone is a worshiper of God and does His will, He hears him." —**John 9:31.** "The Lord is far from the wicked, but He hears the prayer of the righteous." —**Proverbs 15:29.** "The sacrifice of the wicked is an abomination to the Lord, but the prayer of the upright is His delight." —**Proverbs 15:8.**

Nor are the prayers of disobedient born-again believers: "If I regard iniquity in my heart, the Lord will not hear [me]." —**Psalm 66:18.** "One who turns away his ear from hearing the Law, even his prayer is an abomination."—**Proverbs 28:9.** "Ye ask, and receive not, because ye ask amiss, that ye may consume it upon your lusts." —**James 4:3,** KJV.

But God *delights* in the prayers of His faithful followers. "And whatever we ask we receive from Him, because we keep His commandments and do those things that are pleasing in His sight." —**1 John 3:22.** "This is the confidence that we have in Him, that if we ask anything *according to His will,* He hears us." —**1 John 5:14.** "The EYES of the Lord are on the righteous, and His EARS are open to their [vocal, audible] cry." —**Psalm 34:15.**

Whole volumes could be, and have been, written on the subject of prayer, so I won't belabor the subject except to say that "**The Lord's Prayer,**" [41] taught us by Jesus in His magnificent *Sermon on the Mount,* is a perfect model and example for anyone to follow. It is concise yet complete, and absolutely beautiful in expressing the majestic power and glory of God.

On the other hand, and in sharp contrast, Contemplative Prayer falls far short of measuring up as "prayer" at all. For the concept of *prayer* ever and always is defined as an act of **expression** or **communication**, which *presupposes* **thoughts** and **words** as *tools of expression* to communicate thanksgiving or praise, requests or petitions, adoration or confession.

But *by no stretch of the imagination* can the much-touted "Silence" of Contemplative Prayer be considered *"PRAYER" at all—since no THOUGHT is involved.*

On the contrary, it's easy to see that "the Silence" is **only a ploy** used by Satan to *EMPTY the mind of all thoughts,* achieving *a mental void,* thus setting the stage for his demons to begin gradually *filling it,* patiently and cunningly *tutoring us* in a whole new religion, with *NEW* thoughts and a *whole new worldview!*

Of course, from Satan's point of view, this entire scheme is a Masterpiece of Deception! But we—and all THINKING people who *haven't* emptied their minds—must regard Contemplative Prayer not only as **not** "**prayer**" but also as **unchristian, unbiblical, unedifying, unsanctifying,** and *unnecessary!*

As we said before, all teachers of Contemplative Prayer tell us to banish any random thoughts that disturb our meditation. But Trappist monk Thomas Keating goes even further. *He wants his followers in "the Silence" to let go of even* **devout** *thoughts!* He says: "The method consists of letting go of *every thought* during the time of prayer, even *the most devout* thoughts." [42]

Yet, in stark contrast, one engaging in *traditional Christian prayer* finds that <u>devout thoughts are important and desirable</u>. That vital distinction is one of several that *disqualify* Contemplative Prayer as "prayer" at all—*at least in the world as we know it.*

Perhaps you've noticed, having read this far, that **ALL** the mystic teachers agree that—when it comes to Contemplative Prayer and "the Silence"—<u>the enemy is your **MIND**</u>. Your God-given mind must be systematically put into "a kind of *suspended* animation," into "an *altered* state of consciousness." You must deliberately "*silence*" it and "*empty*" it of every *thought* and *feeling*. But that teaching is <u>diametrically opposed</u> to that of the Savior of the world, Jesus Christ, who clearly taught Christians: "You shall LOVE the Lord your God *with all your **heart**, with all your **soul**, and* <u>with all your **MIND**</u>." [43]

- Most people would *resent* a sign at a church reading:
  "Please Check Your BRAIN at the Door."

- They *don't trust* so-called spiritual leaders telling them to
  "Empty Your Mind" so you can achieve **"a mental void."**

- And **why *should*** they trust them—***when the Bible* NEVER** **teaches any such thing?**

So **"Just Say 'NO'"** to the *mystical* "Silence" of Contemplative Prayer— which is clearly **POLES APART** from the traditional prayer we've been taught in the Bible.

3. NONE NEED BE DECEIVED AND MISLED

Those led astray by Contemplative Prayer are going down the path *NOT* of *Gulliver's Travels* but *"Gullibles' Travels."* Yet we need not be gullible and naïve, the pawns and prey of false prophets, the innocent targets of confidence men in priestly robes. No, not at all. We simply must be awake and alert not to take someone's word for anything—even the word of a trusted spiritual leader.

Instead, we must <u>demand the evidence</u> by asking, *"Where does the Bible say that? Where does God teach that in His Word?"* We must require pertinent "chapter and verse" from God's Word for every point of teaching. And if the religious teacher won't—or can't—provide it, we should walk away.

I say *pertinent* "chapter and verse" because spiritual swindlers like to quote one Bible verse that may or may not apply, and then for good measure throw in two or three others that *sound good*—and *ARE* perfectly good Bible verses—but have *absolutely NO relevance* to the teaching being considered! In this book we show that the four main Scripture texts often used by Contemplative Prayer teachers to support their doctrine *really offer NO support at all. So please examine the Scriptural evidence carefully—if there is any!*

For instance, promoters of Contemplative Prayer try hard to convince us that Jesus Himself indulged in the mystical practice of emptying His mind and going into "the Silence." But the Bible absolutely refuses to cooperate in their attempts, for not a single verse in all Scripture even hints that Christ ever did any such thing.

But that doesn't stop them from trying to convince us. They'll grasp at straws by using texts that simply say Jesus "departed to a solitary place; and there He prayed" —**Mark 1:35**. But what does *that* prove? Does it say He *repeatedly uttered a mantra/prayer word?* Does it imply, even indirectly, that He *entered a mental VOID so He could hear the voice of His Father?* No! It says *nothing like that at all.*

You see, Jesus was constantly followed by crowds of people seeking help and healing—so much so that Christ and His apostles "did not even have time to EAT"! —**Mark 6:31** (please read verses **31–34**). Can we blame Jesus and His apostles for trying at times to "get away from it all"?—of course not!

So the supposed "biblical evidence" promoting Contemplative Prayer adds up to NO evidence at all. But please let me share *just one more Bible passage* that will lay to rest, once and for all, the false teaching that Jesus Himself supposedly practiced these mystical things.

JESUS' MOST PASSIONATE PRAYER

This passage—found three times in the Gospels: **Matthew 26:36–46, Mark 14:32–42, and Luke 22:39–46**—depicts a very dramatic moment in the life of Christ, when He, having just finished "The Last Supper" with His apostles, leads them to the Garden of Gethsemane, where He prays perhaps *the most vitally important prayer ever uttered*. This is the Moment of Truth, the Zero Hour, the decisive decision after which *there's NO turning back!*

Christ is going to ask His heavenly Father to "Take this cup"—this excruciating sacrifice—away from Him, *but only if it should be His Father's will*. Otherwise, Jesus will bravely endure it ALL to save us: the shameful humiliation, the brutal beatings, the fatal torture of the Cross.

All of Jesus' prayers, of course, were important. But this prayer—as brief as it was—was undoubtedly the most important one of His earthly ministry. For the awful moment had come on which was hanging the fate of the entire human race—the moment that would decide the destiny of the world! For in this moment Christ still might refuse to drink the cup that guilty sinners deserve. It was not yet too late. He might wipe the dust of this world off His feet and go back to His Father. But—*praise the Lord*—He bravely determined to save mankind at any cost to Himself!

Many profound lessons may be drawn from the drama played out here, but what **three things** pertinent to our present inquiry can we learn from it?

BIBLICAL TRUTH #1.

Ask yourself: Did Christ, in this terrible crisis, take *special* care to follow the procedure prescribed for *Contemplative Prayer?* For instance, did He seek the "solitude" so often mentioned by its teachers and practitioners? Not really. For Christ did not seek complete solitude. **Luke 22:41** says He was withdrawn from His disciples *only "about a stone's throw" away*.

And Jesus knew what the apostles didn't: That there wasn't much time— just "one hour" according to **Matthew 26:40** and **Mark 14:37**—because "a great multitude with swords and clubs" (**Matthew 26:47**) led by Judas, the betrayer, would soon arrive to arrest Him.

Also, we know He definitely was *NOT* concentrating on maintaining whatever degree of solitude even his "stone's throw" degree of distance afforded, because **Mark 14:33–41** tells us *He kept coming back—three times*—to Peter, James, and John, repeatedly urging them to "watch and pray," but with not the slightest hint of *any* mystical practice. And the disciples, for their part, were so overcome with drowsiness they could not resist falling back to sleep.

BIBLICAL TRUTH #2.

Secondly, it's crystal clear that in this vitally important prayer to His Father, our Lord had *NOT emptied His mind*—as Contemplative Prayer teachers so strongly urge! On the contrary, in this extreme emergency, His mind was **crowded** with Thoughts, thoughts expressed in Words. Those brief words of His pitiful anguish are *immortalized forever* on the pages of Scripture. They're *words* and *thoughts* we understand and with which we sympathize.

Jesus, in His hour of anguish, fervently prayed three times:

- **Matthew 14:39** — "O My Father, if it is possible, let this cup pass from Me; nevertheless, not as I will, but as You will."

- **Matthew 14:42** — "Again, a second time, He went away and prayed, saying, 'O My Father, if this cup cannot pass away from Me unless I drink it, Your will be done.'"

- **Matthew 14:43–44** — "And He came and found them asleep again, for their eyes were heavy. So He left them, went away again, and prayed the third time, saying the same words."

Did you get that? The Record says not only that Jesus prayed three times to His Father in heaven, but that He prayed the SAME prayer in *virtually the same exact words!* This means Christ's MIND was alert and active, able to keep those vital thoughts and words clearly in memory. And please note that Christ's repeating His thoughtful prayer bears *NO* resemblance at all to *the mindless repetitive chanting of a "prayer word" or Hindu mantra!*

Thus the Bottom Line is: Jesus' mental processes were *NOT* mystically reduced to "an empty void"—and this most important prayer was ANYTHING BUT *thoughtless, wordless, and mindless!*

BIBLICAL TRUTH #3.

But we see that Jesus—even when plunged into the extremity of this fearful crisis—did *NOT* seek the supposed comfort of a *mystical trance* and absolutely spurned the hellish option of *"altering His consciousness"* in the *self-hypnosis* of "the Silence." At no time was He "out of it"—that is, out of His mind and senses. Much to the contrary, He was all too aware of the gravity of the situation, all too conscious of what was facing Him.

Proof of that stark fact is seen when **Luke 22:44** tells us that "being in agony, . . . **His sweat became like great drops of blood** falling down to the ground." The medical name for "sweating blood" is *hematidrosis*, a rare condition caused most often by severe psychological stress. Note that this feature of Christ's suffering is reported by Luke, the author of the New Testament books of Luke and Acts, a well-educated man who was himself, by profession, a medical doctor. **Colossians 4:14** calls Luke "the beloved physician."

Thus our dear Lord was not only distressed *psychologically* to a high degree, but His whole *physical body* was also. Yet He did not seek the mystical solace that some resort to by going into the "alpha channel" of the brain (discussed below on pages 69–71). Surgeons have even performed operations on patients who were under hypnosis, yet they felt no pain! But Jesus—even under these crucial circumstances—would have nothing to do with it, which indicates that He *never* indulged in it under *any* circumstances. ***Case closed!***

A. DEEP ROOTS IN THE ROMAN CATHOLIC CHURCH

1. The Desert Fathers   ca. 270–500

In the third and fourth centuries, a group of hermits lived in the wilderness of the Middle East (in the desert south and west of Alexandria in Egypt). Dwelling in small isolated communities, those Catholic monks are known to history as the *Desert Fathers* (*and Mothers*—for the few nuns who were with them). The mystic contemplative movement traces its roots back to those monks who promoted the *mantra* as a *prayer tool.*

Daniel Goleman, a proponent of Eastern-style meditation, says that the Desert Fathers from the early centuries of the Catholic Church initially practiced Contemplative Prayer. He states that the mystical practices of these desert monks *strongly resembled the mystical practices of* "their **Hindu** and **Buddhist** renunciate [monkish] brethren several kingdoms to the East." [44]

As we'll see in a few more pages, Goleman is quite right. His voice is just one of a loud chorus telling us that the Desert Fathers unquestionably got their mystical ideas *from the ancient pagan religions of the East.* They certainly didn't get them from the Bible, for there's nothing in God's holy Word that tells of Jesus or His apostles using a mantra and going into the trancelike "Silence" to pray!

2. *The Cloud of Unknowing*   ca. 1375

The Cloud of Unknowing was an early book on Contemplative Prayer written in the late 1300s—about *eight centuries after* the Desert Fathers —by an unknown Catholic monk. It's a book often quoted by teachers and promoters of Contemplative/Centering Prayer.

But Roman Catholic priest John D. Dreher has studied Centering Prayer in depth for years and has sounded many warnings of its dangers. Here he corrects a frequent error in its teaching:

> The book often claimed as a precedent for Centering Prayer is *The Cloud of Unknowing,* by an unknown fourteenth-century English author. But the claim is in vain, for *The Cloud of Unknowing* clearly repudiates the EMPHASIS given in Centering Prayer to *techniques:* "I am trying to make clear with *words* what *experience* teaches more convincingly, that techniques and methods are ultimately *USELESS* for awakening contemplative love."

Dreher concludes by saying, "To see *The Cloud* as pointing us to <u>technique</u> (as Centering Prayer does) is profoundly to *misread* the text." [45]

3. Ignatius of Loyola 1491–1556

We know Loyola today mainly from his founding of the Society of Jesus—the order of the Jesuits—in 1534. One of the missions of the Jesuits was to fight the battles of the Roman Catholic Church against the Protestants, in what is now termed the Counter-Reformation.

For our purposes Ignatius's contribution lies in the creation of his little book called *Spiritual Exercises,* which provided—and *still* provides to this day—specifications for the mental and spiritual conditioning of the Jesuits. Richard Foster's "Spiritual Disciplines" in his book seem to draw heavily upon Ignatius.

In fact, the chapters in Richard Foster's best-seller, *Celebration of Discipline* (1978), are on what he calls the twelve **"Spiritual Disciplines"** [46]—*a reverberating echo* of the title and content of Loyola's book, written more than four centuries before, and a similarity more by design than mere chance.

It's also interesting that, if you Google *Ignatius Loyola's spiritual exercises* on the Internet you'll find the Wikipedia article that tells us:

> Beginning in the 1980s, ***Protestants*** have had a <u>growing interest in</u> <u>[Loyola's]</u> *Spiritual Exercises.* There are recent (2006) adaptations that are specific to **Protestants** that *EMPHASIZE* the exercises as a ***school of Contemplative Prayer!*** [47]

4. Thomas Merton 1915–1968

Thomas Merton was a world-renowned Trappist monk who lived at the Abbey of Gethsemani in Kentucky from 1941 to his death in 1968. He became so enamored with the mysticism of Eastern religions that eventually he confessed:

> Asia, Zen [Buddhism], Islam, all these things come together in my life. It would be madness for me to attempt to create a monastic life for myself by excluding all these. I would be less a monk. [48]

Nevertheless, at one time in his life Merton reached the point when he thought he would have to leave Christianity to become a true mystic. But when he met a Hindu swami, Dr. Bramachari, Bramachari "left a deep influence on Thomas Merton" for whom Merton had "great respect and deep REVERENCE." [49] Bramachari told Merton he could find *this same mysticism* within the confines of *"Christian"* mystics.

Merton concluded, much through Bramachari's influence, that if he had an "openness to Buddhism, to Hinduism, to those great Asian [mystical] traditions," [50] he would be able to incorporate those into his own Christian tradition. And Thomas Merton gave many talks and wrote many books to advance his mystical beliefs before his untimely death (he was accidentally electrocuted while visiting Thailand).

Christian writer and researcher Ray Yungen tells us:

> What Martin Luther King was to the civil rights movement and what Henry Ford was to the automobile, Thomas Merton was to Contemplative Prayer. . . . Merton took it out of its [monastery and nunnery] setting and made it available to, and popular with, the masses. . . . Thomas Merton has influenced the Christian mystical movement more than any [other] person of recent decades. [51]

Richard Foster, of course, agrees, calling Merton's book *Contemplative Prayer* "a *must* book." [52]

5. Thomas Keating 1923–
6. Basil Pennington 1931–2005

"Centering Prayer" originated in St. Joseph's Abbey, a Trappist monastery in Spencer, Massachusetts. In the mid-seventies, Trappist Abbot (the head monk) Thomas Keating asked the monks,

> Could we put the Christian tradition into a form that would be accessible to people . . . who have been instructed in an *Eastern* technique and might be inspired to *return* to their *Christian* roots if they knew there was <u>something similar</u> in the Christian tradition? [53]

Trappist monks Basil Pennington and William Menniger took up the challenge along with Abbot Keating, and "Centering Prayer" (the age-old Contemplative Prayer with a new name) is the result. In a few short years this mystical practice—by *either* name—has spread all over the world.

It should also be added that

> during the twenty years (1961–1981) when Keating was abbot, St. Joseph's Abbey held dialogues with *Buddhist* and *Hindu* representatives, and *a Zen Buddhist master* gave a week-long retreat to the monks. A former Trappist monk who had become a *Transcendental Meditation teacher* also gave a session to the monks. [54]

7. Henri Nouwen 1932–1996

A Catholic theologian and mystic who has gained popularity and respect in Christian circles, akin to that of Thomas Merton, is the now deceased Henri Nouwen (pronounced "NOW-en"). A popular author and academic,

Nouwen taught at the University of Notre Dame, Harvard, and Yale. Many pastors and professors are attracted to his deep thinking. [55]

In fact, one of his biographers revealed that in a 1994 survey of thirty-four hundred U.S. **Protestant** church leaders, Dutch-born Nouwen ranked second only to Billy Graham in influence among them. [56]

On two separate occasions, megachurch minister Rick Warren referred to one of Nouwen's books on his Web site for pastors, saying: "My wife, Kay, recommends this book: [She says,] *'It's a short book, but it hits at the heart of the minister. . . . I highlighted almost every word!'* " [57]

The book recommended is Nouwen's *In the Name of Jesus*. Nouwen devotes an entire chapter of that book to Contemplative Prayer, saying:

> Through the discipline of Contemplative Prayer, Christian leaders have to *learn to listen* to the voice of love. . . . For Christian leadership to be *truly fruitful* in the future, **a movement from the MORAL to the MYSTICAL is REQUIRED**. [58]

8. Brennan Manning 1930–

A former Catholic priest, Brennan Manning has authored such popular titles as *The Ragamuffin Gospel* and *The Signature of Jesus*. After being treated for alcoholism and leaving the Franciscan Order in 1982, he married Roslyn Ann Walker. The marriage has since ended in divorce, but his popularity as a writer and speaker continues to grow *despite* his proclamation of "another" gospel. [59]

Regarding what seems to be "another gospel," Manning in his 2003 book *Above All*, makes this statement concerning the atonement:

> [T]he god whose moods alternate between graciousness and fierce anger . . . the god who exacts the last drop of blood from his Son so that his just anger, evoked by sin, may be appeased, is not the god revealed by and in Jesus Christ. And if he is not the god of Jesus, he *does not exist.* [60]

In the last ten years, he has become a popular speaker in many Protestant evangelical churches. His admirers include popular Christian singers like Amy Grant and Michael Card and popular Christian authors like Max Lucado and Philip Yancey. Yancey endorsed Manning to all his own readers by proclaiming, "I consider Brennan Manning my *spiritual director* in the school of grace." [61]

But apparently even "spiritual directors" can have "feet of clay."

In 2005 *Christianity Today* called Manning's book *The Ragamuffin Gospel* a "spiritual classic." Yet after they published the later article "A

Coward Who Stayed to Help"—which was Manning's story of his alleged heroics assisting victims during the Hurricane Katrina disaster—they had to publish a **retraction** five days later stating that *Manning had lied*. In a voice message to *Christianity Today* he blithely said, "The essential truth: I lied." [62]

B. Earlier Roots in Ancient EASTERN Religions

I enjoy studying and writing about Comparative Religion. That means I face the task of comparing and contrasting different belief systems of the world—with the inevitable result that among the communities of faith *some* look *better* and *some* look *worse* than others. I must try, without being mean or excessively critical, to give readers the facts. I mention this here because in this study I frequently refer to "the ancient *Eastern* religions" of Hinduism and Buddhism—which lie in strong *CONTRAST* to Christianity.

1. When East Meets West

Born in India, Rudyard Kipling (1865–1936) was a British poet and storyteller instead of a theologian. But two lines from his "Ballad of East and West" seem almost prophetic when describing *the clash of cultures*—and *the world of difference* between Christianity and Eastern religions:

"Oh, East is East, and West is West, and never the twain shall meet,
till Earth and Sky stand presently at God's great Judgment Seat."

Hinduism and Buddhism *DIFFER* with Christianity at an absolutely BASIC level—*and they differ even with each other!*

On the one hand, Hinduism is decidedly *polytheistic* with countless gods and goddesses for almost everything in nature, though—ironically enough— Hindus are also strongly *monistic* or *pantheistic,* believing that ALL is ONE ultimate reality, or essence, or god called Brahman.

On the other hand, Buddhism *denies* and *rejects* the notion of a personal god or creator so that it is basically *atheistic.* Yet it believes and teaches a philosophy that ALL is ONE—*including* whatever concept of a supreme being one may have. Thus it is, like Hinduism, also *monistic* or *pantheistic.*

Reginald A. Ray, professor of Buddhist Studies at Naropa University, wrote a 2001 article with the intriguing title "Religion Without God," in which he said:

Unlike most of the other world religions, Buddhism *denies* the ultimate existence of any "God" or deity. . . . [Yet, paradoxically,] Buddhists everywhere believe in an "*unseen world*" inhabited by a full range of gods, demi-gods, *spirits*, ghosts and *demons*. . . . The Buddhist approach states that *what is ultimately required for human fulfillment is a perfection of being **that is found in who WE already ARE.*** [63]

In other words, Buddhism proclaims that <u>nothing outside yourself is needed for salvation</u>—a worldview *worlds apart from Christianity!*

So it is truly a marvel—and a great irony—that the very *latest* form of supposedly "Christian" prayer was born *long ago and far away* in the **pagan** lands of the mystic Far East: India, Tibet, China, and later, Japan.

But teachers and proponents of Contemplative Prayer try desperately hard to brainwash people with the idea that this mystic meditation is somehow a "Christian" practice—yet *their own words* prove how *fallacious* this idea is!

For the mystical prayer method promoted by Richard Foster and others like Catholic monks Thomas Merton and Thomas Keating can indeed be shown to have very strong—and obvious—links to *EASTERN* mysticism. And in their flood of writings, *over and over again,* they themselves say the same thing! So their own words may reasonably be used against them. Let's look at a few examples of these for proof.

Thomas Keating and Basil Pennington, two Trappist monks, collaborated on the book *Finding Grace at the Center* and gave this advice:

> We should not hesitate to take ***the fruit of the age-old wisdom of the EAST*** and "capture" it for Christ. Indeed, those of us who are in **ministry** should make the necessary effort to <u>acquaint ourselves with as many of these *EASTERN* techniques as possible.</u> . . .
>
> Many **Christians** who take their prayer life seriously have been <u>greatly helped by</u> Yoga, Zen, TM [Transcendental Meditation] and similar [Eastern] practices. [64]

All through their books, Keating and Pennington talk about finding "the True Self," finding out who we really are. What exactly *IS* the True Self? Keating states, "God and our true Self are *NOT separate.* Though we are not God, *God and our true Self **are the same thing**.*" [65]

Yet the concept of "the True Self" originated in **Hinduism**. According to Catholic author and broadcaster Johnnette Benkovic, the Hindus believe:

> The Self is none other than Brahman or god. . . . The True Self is God. The "I" which I consider myself to be is in reality the *not-self.* This "not-self" is caught in a world of illusion, ignorance, and bondage. You must *lose* your personal ego-consciousness into god. You must say, "**I am Brahman.**" [66]

Also, Keating gives this frank and revealing advice to Christian pastors who seek to guide their church members into the *mystical* realms:

In order to guide persons having this experience [divine oneness], Christian spiritual directors may need to **dialogue with *EASTERN* teachers** in order to *get a fuller understanding.* [67]

Popular Catholic priest and author Henri Nouwen, who was chosen to write the Foreword for Thomas Ryan's book *Disciplines for Christian Living*, *reveals his **OWN** love* for ***EASTERN*** religions as he pays this tribute:

[T]he author shows a *wonderful openness* to the *gifts* of **Buddhism**, **Hinduism**, and **Moslem** religion. He discovers *their great wisdom for the spiritual life of the Christian.* . . . Ryan [the author] *went to **India*** to learn from *spiritual traditions other than his own*. He brought home ***many treasures*** and offers them to us in the book. [68]

Trappist monk and mystic Thomas Merton openly confessed, "I'm deeply impregnated with Sufism." [69] Sufism is ***Islamic mysticism!*** And yet, Richard Foster says of Merton:

Thomas Merton has perhaps done *more* than any other twentieth-century figure to make the life of *prayer* widely known and understood. . . . His interest in *contemplation* led him to investigate *prayer forms in **EASTERN*** religion [that is, pagan religions such as Hinduism, Buddhism, and Islamic Sufism]. **Zen masters from Asia** [70] regarded him as the preeminent authority on ***THEIR kind of prayer*** in the United States. [71]

Ultimately, Merton's mystical experiences made him a kindred spirit and co-mystic with those in ***EASTERN*** religions. He did not flinch from declaring:

I believe that by openness to **Buddhism**, to **Hinduism**, and to those *great* **Asian** [mystical] traditions, we stand a *wonderful* chance of learning more about the potentiality of our own Christian traditions. [72]

One biographer, attempting to spread Merton's mystic message after his death, tells us that Thomas Merton *"quaffed [drank] eagerly from the **BUDDHIST** cup in his journey to the **EAST**."* [73]

Virtually all the many "spiritual leaders" that Foster praises in his books have strong leanings toward and interest in ***EASTERN* mysticism,** but Catholic monk Thomas Merton goes so far as to admit: "I think *I couldn't understand Christian teaching* the way I do if it were *NOT* in the light of *Buddhism*." [74] He also unashamedly expressed such views as: "*I see NO contradiction between Buddhism and Christianity.* . . . *I intend to become as good a Buddhist as I can.*" [75]

And Richard Foster, when he first published *Celebration of Discipline* in 1978, wrote:

How depressing for a university student, seeking to know the *Christian* teaching on meditation, to discover that there are *so few living masters* of Contemplative Prayer and that nearly all the serious writings on the subject are *seven or more centuries old*. No wonder he or she turns to **Zen**, **Yoga**, or **TM**. [76]

This statement by Foster is quite revealing, stating that there was little or no teaching on the *mystical meditation of Contemplative Prayer* in **Christian** ranks, for Bible scholars **knew** that God's Word strongly **DAMNS** all spiritualistic and mystical practices. And there were "so few living masters" besides a Catholic monk like Thomas Merton, for fellow Catholic mystics like the Desert Fathers and Ignatius Loyola had died centuries ago. The Protestant Reformers, too, following their principle of *sola scriptura* (Scripture alone), would have nothing to do with such a non-biblical teaching.

But the real "dead giveaway" in Foster's statement is the last part, where he admits that those seeking to learn such **OCCULT** practices would be driven *NOT* to the Bible but to **ancient EASTERN teachings** like Zen (from Buddhism), or Yoga (from Hinduism), or TM (Transcendental Meditation, from the so-called New Age)! *Verrry interesting, indeed!*

Even in his bold attempt to sell *Eastern mysticism* to the *Christian* community, Richard Foster does not shrink from mentioning his dangerous affinity for "the New Age"—which has strong links to the ancient religions of the East—in these candid words:

"*We of the New Age can RISK going against the tide.*" [77]

It's both bold and revealing that Richard Foster, in his praise for Catherine de Hueck Doherty's ministry, actually admits that the title of her book is, *Poustinia: Christian Spirituality of the **EAST** for **WESTERN** Man.* [78] This leaves little doubt as to the **source** for this type of prayer.

In her book *A Quiet Revolution*, Jodi Mailander Farrell tells the truth when she writes: "***Sparked by EASTERN meditative techniques,*** today's version of Centering Prayer is bent on ***stilling*** **the mind.**" The more one learns about Contemplative Prayer and its mystical "Silence," the more one is moved to ask: "Is this an ***EASTERN*** **yoga type of thing** with a 'Christian' sticker slapped on the side?"

For those still skeptical, Episcopal priest Tilden Edwards, the co-founder of one of America's largest centers for teaching Contemplative Prayer, THE SHALEM INSTITUTE in Washington D.C., explicitly admits that "this *mystical* stream *[Contemplative Prayer] is* **the Western BRIDGE to Far Eastern spirituality.**" [79] How much more clear can this be?

2. CP and TM Are Mystical TWINS!

That Contemplative Prayer—in both its panentheistic **beliefs** and mantra-meditation **methods**—was *derived from* and *influenced by* Hinduism and Buddhism seems so obvious to me as to need no further proof. The abundant evidence indeed speaks for itself.

But don't take my word for it: When, in a court of law, cool heads assessed all the facts in a case involving the **EASTERN** mystical practice of "Transcendental Meditation," the judges decided the same way I—and many others—would have.

PLEASE NOTE: Courts in the United States have *legally ruled* that Transcendental Meditation is *NOT* a secular discipline—it is Hindu religion. Therefore, it cannot be taught in public schools (as they were trying to do) without violating the separation of church and state. [80]

That legal decision, of course, was both just and wise, for TM was inspired by Hinduism and is permeated by that religion in almost every detail. Due to TM's ancient history, there was nothing new about it when it was swept into uncommon popularity in the 1960s by Maharishi Mahesh Yogi (1917–2008), a Hindu guru who arrived in England from India to peddle "mantra meditation." His fortunes grew when, in 1967, he was embraced with enthusiasm by the Beatles—who even traveled to India to visit his TM training center.

But, for those who have examined it, *Contemplative Prayer is so close to Transcendental Meditation as to be almost identical.* One practitioner very knowledgeable in *both* of those mystic methods, Catholic priest Finbarr Flanagan, says: *"Centering Prayer* **IS** *Transcendental Meditation* masquerading in a Christian dress." [81]

Further, in that same article which Flanagan called "Centering Prayer: *Transcendental Meditation for the Christian Market,"* he was bold to say: "As an ex-TM mediator, I find it hard to see *ANY* differences between Centering Prayer and Transcendental Meditation"—a sentiment shared by many with the same knowledge. The *many* similarities between Centering Prayer and Transcendental Meditation are indisputably striking, so let's look at them:

SPIRITUAL TWINS

A. Both CP and TM use a 20-minute meditation.

B. Both CP and TM use a mantra to erase all thoughts and feelings.

> C. Both CP and TM teach that in this meditation you pick up <u>vibrations.</u>
>
> D. Both CP and TM claim that this meditation will give you <u>more peace and less tension.</u>
>
> E. Both CP and TM teach you how to reach <u>a mental void</u> or <u>altered level of consciousness.</u>
>
> F. Both CP and TM have the common goal of finding <u>your god-center.</u>

Regarding the Table Above, Please Note:

- As for (**A**) above, the official Web site for The Transcendental Meditation Program [82] spells out a **"20-minute session twice each day"**—as does Benedictine monk John Main,[83] Trappist monk Abbot Thomas Keating,[84] *Newsweek* magazine,[85] and virtually *every other teacher* of Contemplative Prayer on record.

- In regard to (**C**) *vibrations,* Keating says, "As you go to a deeper level of reality, you begin to pick up *vibrations* that were there all the time but not perceived."[86] Pennington also speaks of "physical *vibrations* that are helpful."[87] *"Good Vibrations!"* are *common* TM and New Age language.

- Using (**B**) *mantras* and (**E**) reaching *a mental void* are both also New Age, not Christian at all. In fact, for Catholics who respect the authority of their latest official *Catechism,* reaching "a mental void" is described in the *Catechism* as one of the "*erroneous* notions of prayer."[88]

- And finally, (**F**) finding your "god-center" *within* yourself is the false and pagan worldview of *panentheism*—to be dealt with below.

  So what do all these facts tell us? At least **three things:**

First, Transcendental Meditation has been judged in a court of law to be not a secular discipline but instead found to be "Hindu religion."

Second, Contemplative/Centering Prayer and Transcendental Meditation are **identical images** of each other.

Third, since **TM** = Hindu religion, and
    since **CP** = **TM** in all major respects,[89]

THEN, in conclusion, CP *ALSO* = *Hindu religion!*

A 2005 book titled *In the Sphere of Silence* is a metaphysical manual on *mystic meditation* and *altered states of consciousness*. In it, author Vijay Eswaran teaches: "The Sphere of Silence, if it is practiced properly, is *a very powerful tool*. . . . It is through **SILENCE** that you find your true being." His Web site adds that his book "stems from the *ancient **Hindu*** concept, especially from ***yogic*** traditions, of practicing *mouna* (**silence**)." [90]

We can only wish that all clergy were honest enough to admit that while Contemplative Prayer and its "Silence" are quite ***common*** to Eastern religion, they are ***foreign*** to Scripture—*and therefore definitely **NOT** Christian*.

C. Modern Sources in PROTESTANT Proponents

So far we've seen that ***mystic meditation***—using mantras to empty one's mind to engage the spirit voices speaking in Contemplative Prayer—has a *very long history* going all the way back to the ancient pagan religions of the East. Much later, around A.D. 300–500, the Desert Fathers picked it up and passed it on to other monks in the Roman Catholic Church. It stayed there, confined almost exclusively within the walls of monasteries, convents, and abbeys until Loyola in 1534, and, much later, modern monks like Merton and Keating tried hard to spread it more widely.

But there was still a strong resistance to those very mystical experiences God so clearly condemns. The **Protestant Reformers**—Martin Luther, who founded the Lutheran Church; John Calvin, who founded the Presbyterian Church; John Wesley, who founded the Methodist Church; and others like them—recognized the danger and would have nothing to do with any of it. So the proponents of Contemplative Prayer had a problem: How to penetrate and infiltrate the Protestant/Evangelical churches. And as Fate would have it, *they found the solution they needed in a young man named Richard Foster!*

1. Richard Foster and the Quaker Connection

In 1978 Richard Foster wrote a book called *Celebration of Discipline*, which has, in the thirty-plus years since, sold over one million copies. It was honored in the year 2000 by the influential magazine *Christianity Today*, which named it **"One of the TOP TEN Books of the Century"!**

Over the years, Foster has written or edited several other books and worked actively as a speaker at pastor's meetings to promote his "baby" of Contemplative Prayer. Perhaps calling the baby *his* is a bit one-sided, for certainly many others have been involved. But still, there are those who feel quite justified in calling Richard Foster the "father" of this mystical movement—at least in its **modern** manifestation in Protestant and Evangelical circles.

Yet for Foster this work must have seemed natural and easy, almost as if he was destined by Fate to this, his "calling" in life. I say this because Richard Foster is a **Quaker**. Born and raised in a Quaker home, he has lived as a lifelong member of the "Society of Friends," and when it was time for college, he chose GEORGE FOX UNIVERSITY, a Quaker school in Oregon. The Official Quaker Web site tells us that "perhaps the best known Quaker in the world today is Richard J. Foster." [91]

And later in life when he hungered for outside reading, for some reason he immersed himself very deeply—and almost exclusively—in Catholic mystical writers.

Those two influences in his life have had a profound effect. We can all understand the effect of the Catholic mystics, for it shows itself so strongly in all of Foster's later work. But let me share a little about the Quaker religion, which is *so very different from that of most Christian churches,*[92] and you'll see why it's such an important factor in this connection. To some extent, *"Are Quakers Christian?"* is still an open question. One authoritative source says:

> Although *outsiders* usually regard the movement as a Christian de-nomination, *not all Quakers* see themselves as Christians; some regard themselves as members of a **universal** religion that (for *historical* rea-sons) has many Christian elements. . . . Quakers are willing to learn from *all other* faiths and churches. —BBC [93]

Another source tells us: "There is a **strong MYSTICAL component** to Quaker belief." —OCRT (see endnote 93)

In order to keep this study short, since so much could be said, I want to focus on just **three** of the Quakers' beliefs and practices:

a. Their uniform practice of "the Silence"
b. Their worldviews of *universalism* and *panentheism*
c. Their *setting aside* God's written revelation in the Bible
    in favor of *direct, personal* enlightenment

A helpful overview is found in **Harper's Encyclopedia of Mystical and Paranormal Experience,** which tells us that Quaker theology "stresses a *personal,* almost *mystical* knowledge of God and the workings of the Lord's **'inner light' WITHIN ALL people.**" It adds that George Fox himself taught:

> Faith is based **SOLELY** on *FIRSTHAND* knowledge of Christ as a liv-ing, *personal* reality, *NOT* on logic, reasoning, historical reporting, **or even Scripture.** This empirical proof came to be called **the Quaker Way**: the idea that *worshippers need NOT consult preachers OR the Bible*

to receive knowledge of the Holy Spirit—the so-called **"inner light** of Christ" present **IN every** human heart. [94]

The Quakers—also known as the "Religious Society of Friends"—began in England in the 1650s, a time of religious and political turmoil there. Its founder was **George Fox** (1624–1691), who at that time suffered severe spiritual depression from the spectacle of human suffering and from the doctrine of predestination [95] he heard preached from Puritan pulpits.

Thoroughly disgusted by such preaching, Fox, in strong reaction, turned against organized religion in general, and preachers and preaching in particular. The great church historian Kenneth Scott Latourette adds a bit more background information on the person through whom the Quakers originated:

> By temperament a *mystic,* he was eager for **direct** and unhindered access to God. . . . [Fox] would follow and have others follow the **Inner Light**. [96]

Let me continue now by addressing the three points listed above.

a. The Quakers' Practice of "the Silence"

> *They do not have clergy* or rituals, and their meetings for worship are **often held in SILENCE**. . . . Quaker communal worship consists of **SILENT WAITING**, with participants *contributing* as the spirit *moves* them. . . . In a Quaker meeting for worship a group of people sits in a room in **SILENCE** for an hour. From time to time someone may speak briefly, but sometimes the entire hour may pass without a word being spoken. . . . The people present try to create **an** *internal* **SILENCE**—a SILENCE *inside* their head [mind]. They do this by stopping everyday thoughts. Quakers believe that if they **wait SILENTLY for God** in this way there will be times when *God will speak directly to them.* —BBC (see endnote **93**)

> *Most* meetings are *unprogrammed*. That is, they are held in **SILENCE**. Attendees *speak* when *moved* to do so. Elsewhere, services have *programmed* orders of worship, usually led by a pastor. They usually arrange the congregation in a *square* or *circle,* so that each person is aware of everyone else. —OCRT (see endnote **93**)

b. The Quakers' False Worldview

NOTE: *Pantheism* is the pagan belief that "ALL is God." *Panentheism* is its twin that says, "God is IN everyone and everything." The Quakers—like the Hindus, Buddhists, and New Agers—are *panentheists*.

Quakers believe that there is something of **God IN everybody**. —BBC (see endnote **93**)

The **HEART** of Quakerism is the belief in **an Inner Light**, a part of God's spirit that **dwells IN every soul**. —OCRT (see endnote **93**)

Church historian Latourette again shares a key piece of information on Fox's theology right here: "Fox and others insisted that **EVERY** man who comes into the world is illuminated by an inner light which is Christ." [97]

Pastor Ken Silva wisely observes that the above view held by "Fox and others" makes Quakers guilty of teaching not only *panentheism,* but also the equally false worldview of *universalism* (that is, belief in *universal salvation for ALL*—including Osama bin Laden and all other mass murderers). For **IF** this alleged Inner Light is *already* within **EVERY** man, then it negates any need for **anyone** to be regenerated or "born again." [98]

Such a worldview *completely cancels any need for the gospel of Christ!*

c. The Quakers' Setting Aside the Bible

Quakers do **NOT** regard **ANY** book as being the actual "word of God." . . . The Bible is **NOT** regarded as the only guide for conduct and belief. Doubt and questioning are *valuable tools* for spiritual growth. **ALL human beings** can have a **DIRECT** [that is, **mystical**] **experience** of God. —BBC (see endnote **93**)

Apparently George Fox's **personal** "direct experience," referred to in the line above, failed to help his Christian faith. For he rudely shoved the Truth of the Bible to a place *far* **secondary** to his own mystical "Inner Light."

In his fine work *Christianity Through the Centuries,* noted Church historian Dr. Earle Cairns tells us that:

The Quakers appeared on the English religious scene during the chaotic period of the Civil War and the Commonwealth. **They SET ASIDE the doctrines** of an organized church **and the Bible** as the sole and final revelation of God's will *in favor of the doctrine of* **the Inner Light**, by which they meant that the Holy Spirit can give *immediate* and *direct* knowledge of God **APART FROM the Bible**. [99]

Thus the Quaker persuasion—with its constant emphasis on the "Silence," with its *mystical* expectation of "God's voice," with its insistence that ALL HUMANITY has God or Christ **within,** with its *aversion* to the Bible and *lack* of any *doctrinal* teaching—is an "unconventional" church, to say the least!

Seeing this lifelong background, in which Richard Foster was immersed and nurtured, helps us now to understand **WHY** he did **NOT** think the continual practice of wordless, thoughtless, mindless "prayer" while in a deep, intentional **silence** to be **downright strange**—as most thoughtful people almost invariably do upon first encountering the idea.

In an interview in the magazine *Christianity Today,* Foster was asked:

"How did you start to become interested in **Spiritual Formation** in a more focused way?" He replied:

> *I don't know exactly why*—I *instinctively* went to the **OLD** writers. I just felt like Augustine's *Confessions* and [Saint] Teresa's *Interior Castle*—this was **real meat.** [100]

Perhaps almost anything might seem like "real meat" to one not fed with the Word of God—which, by the way, *is much more "OLD" and authoritative* than the writers Foster cited. Any reader of Foster's books—which read like a *"Who's Who"* of contemplative Catholics and other mystical writers—is bound to notice *how **SELDOM** the Bible is referenced in comparison with those!*

Therefore, those two influences—Quakerism and mystical writers, both of which are un-Christian and un-Scriptural—were clearly (and unfortunately) the **sources** of Richard Foster's thinking and worldview.

2. Dallas Willard 1935–

Willard has been called Richard Foster's "twin" because of the similarity of their mystical beliefs and also because years ago they both found themselves at the same little Quaker church in the San Fernando Valley of Southern California. Willard and his wife attended there when Foster arrived as the young pastor just out of seminary. Dallas Willard seemed to become the younger man's mentor. He has written a number of books in the contemplative field and still exerts some influence in the mystical movement. But he maintains a lower profile and seems content to stay quietly within the academic world as a professor at the University of Southern California.

3. Rick Warren 1954–

Rick Warren is pastor of Saddleback Church—a megachurch with twenty-two thousand members and a mailing list of over eighty thousand names—in Lake Forest (located in Orange County, California). His book *The Purpose-Driven Life* sold *nearly thirty million copies* and was "on the must-read list for every pastor." [101]

But in his first book, *The Purpose-Driven Church,* also very popular, Warren praises a number of movements he believes God has "raised up" to remedy "a neglected purpose" in Christianity. One of those he mentions is the **Spiritual Formation** movement, which promotes Contemplative Prayer. Warren names Richard Foster and Dallas Willard as leaders of this movement and declares that this movement has a *"valid message for the church"* and has *"given the church of Christ a wake-up call."* [102]

Statements like these, as well as much other evidence, prove that Warren strongly approves of and promotes Contemplative Prayer. And Christian writer Ray Yungen warns that if a Protestant leader *as influential as Rick Warren promotes it,* this guarantees that Contemplative Prayer will be promoted on an enormous scale. [103] And we already see it infiltrating mainstream Christianity to a frightening degree.

D. "The Emerging Church"

The so-called "Emerging" or "Emergent" Church is a radical, revolutionary attempt to renew our worship patterns and to change the way we "do" church. In their attempt to revamp religion in the twenty-first century, leaders of the Emerging Church movement regard nothing as sacred and no change as "going too far."

The devil's strategy is very crafty in targeting TWO important—and vulnerable—elements or groups within God's church: The *first attack* is aimed at **the church LEADERS themselves**. They are vulnerable because conscientious ministers, pastors, and priests are always searching for new, effective ways to improve their work and convert more souls, and Spiritual Formation seems to promise a fresh approach.

The *second target* is the **church YOUTH—the young people** who, as the next generation, are the *future* of the church. They are vulnerable because even those youth raised in Christian homes may, when reaching the age of accountability, become bored and tired of the traditional worship of their parents' ways. Then they begin seeking new paths of "spirituality" and constantly look for anything that takes them "out of the ruts" and into some novel experience.

Satan is only too willing to accommodate these two distinctive and essential groups. To the **professional church leaders** he furnishes new perspectives, new ideas, new methods. and then markets them under the new-sounding, cutting-edge title of "The Emerging Church." He sells his ideas on a wholesale basis, distributing them so widely through every segment of today's religion, reaching not just the New Agers, but also *ALL* the Protestant denominations—all the evangelicals, all the charismatics—as well as all the Roman Catholics.[104] He teaches those church leaders about his Spiritual Formation and Contemplative Prayer in many books, and in many well-publicized and well-attended seminars and workshops that even busy pastors can attend in a weekend retreat.

And he takes pretty much the same approach to **ensnare the young people** who are seeking to freshen their spiritual experience. *Thousands* of

youth and **youth leaders** from *all faiths*—along with young unbelievers with no faith—have already congregated at **"spiritual retreats"** to be taught the techniques of Contemplative Prayer. Since Centering Prayer is so simple, it doesn't take long for even beginners to get the basic idea. And like the *Pied Piper of Hamelin* in the legendary story, the seductive voices of diabolical "spirit entities" in "the Silence" steal away the hearts and minds of *our precious youth—the future of our church!*

The Emerging Church is <u>clearly **market driven**</u>, with a philosophy of **"Whatever works . . ."** and a compromising, willing tendency to **conform to the *CULTURE*** around it.

Personal Experience Trumps Doctrine!

It's sad but true that in today's world **church growth** has become the all-important <u>measuring stick</u> for "successful" Christianity and has given birth to the *market-driven* church, the *seeker-friendly* church, the *Emergent* Church—but *NOT* the *Scripture-faithful* church! The Emergent Church is led by liberal, loose, and freethinking pastors who have little regard for the Word of God. For them and the sheep in their flock who follow them, personal *experience trumps doctrine,* and *feelings win out over* **the Bible!**

But if doctrine is not important, then you can believe whatever you want. If doctrine is not important, then who cares what God says about sin and salvation? And if doctrines are not important, then we can join with all those other churches on things about which we basically agree (which isn't very much at all).

It seems that Emerging Church leaders don't believe in church doctrines. But there **IS**, after all, **ONE** <u>rock solid doctrine</u> about which they feel very strongly, and that is that **"Doctrines Don't Matter!"**

The movement is still so new that no real uniformity is seen as yet—with variations seen among local "emerging" congregations—but *five "common denominators"* are the following:

- **Highly "creative" approaches** to worship and spiritual reflection, involving everything from **contemporary** (loud rock) music and films to other **more ancient** customs like Contemplative Prayer.

- **Preaching and teaching of God's Word** is *DOWNPLAYED* and presented *no more often* than, say, **dramatic "skits"** on stage.

- **A "flexible" approach to theology** whereby *individual differences* in **belief and morality** are *easily accepted.*

- **A strong desire to RE-ANALYZE the Bible** against the context into which it was written and thereby *diminish* its application to today.

● An all-encompassing attempt to provide a "sensory experience" to worshipers through **ALL** their senses: *sight, sound, smell, taste, and touch*—rather than a mere intellectual appeal to their minds.

The Emerging Church Movement is still rather young, but already three leaders have emerged *(if I dare use that word!)*: Dan Kimball, Robert Webber, and Brian McLaren.

1. DAN KIMBALL

Dan Kimball is pastor of the Vintage Faith Church in Santa Cruz, California and wrote the book called *The Emerging Church: Vintage Christianity for New Generations.* Popular pastor Rick Warren wrote a glowing Foreword to Kimball's book and praised it highly—so you know where *he* stands on this new movement!

Kimball believes the world we live in now is much different from ever before and now includes many different religions. In his book *The Emerging Church,* he put it this way:

> In a **post-Christian** world, **pluralism** is the norm. Buddhism, Wicca, Christianity, Islam, Hinduism, or an eclectic *[that is, a choice or mixture made from many different options]* **blend**—it's all part of the soil. [105]

He further claims that "the basis for learning has **SHIFTED** from *logic* and *rational*" to "the realm of *experience*" and the *"mystical."* [106] That sounds *somehow familiar!*

"ANCIENT-FUTURE" WORSHIP

Kimball likes to use the term *vintage*—he even named his church "the Vintage Faith Church" because he believes *vintage* refers to something good from the past. Another term popular in the Emerging Church is *Ancient-Future,* coined by Robert Webber, a professor for thirty-two years at Wheaton College, Billy Graham's old *alma mater.*

2. ROBERT WEBBER 1933–2007

What Webber means by "Ancient-Future" is that in order to go *ahead,* we must go *back to the mystics* and learn from them. And he gave a long list of books he recommended, many of them written by mystics mentioned on these pages. The Ancient-Future concept just reinforces a mystical leaning in the Emergent Church that was already there. Webber showers *mysticism* and its teachers with unbridled praise in these glowing words:

> The *primary* source of spiritual reading is the Bible. But we now recognize that in our love for Scripture *we DARE not AVOID the*

MYSTICS. . . . More and more people are turning to *the great work of the mystics*. . . . To *immerse* ourselves in *these great works* is to allow our vision to be expanded by *a great TREASURE* of spirituality. . . . The *value* of all these books are *indispensable* to spirituality. Those who *NEGLECT* these works do so to their *HARM,* and those who read them do so for their inspiration and spiritual growth. [107]

So the Ancient-Future church does all it can to promote *mysticism* among its adherents. And it is also very strongly *ecumenical* in its aims, seeking to unite all churches, all religions into *ONE unified global body*. Webber quite openly states the future **GOAL:**

A goal for evangelicals in the post-modern world is to *accept* **DIVERSITY** as a historical reality, but to *seek* UNITY in the midst of it. This perspective will allow us to see Catholic, Orthodox, and Protestant churches as *various forms of the ONE true church*—ALL based on apostolic teaching and authority, finding *common ground* in the faith expressed by *classical* Christianity. [108]

Thus we see that the "Ancient-Future" church looks both ways:

Looking to the *Past,* it seeks to revive and resurrect the ancient *mysticism* of the Eastern pagan religions of Hinduism and Buddhism.

Looking to the *Future,* it seeks to realize its dream of *ecumenism* by achieving a unified worldwide religion—even at the costly risk of *diluting doctrine,* by *watering down* Bible teaching, and by *compromising* God's Truth.

So when Kimball claims: "We are simply going back to a VINTAGE form of worship *which has been around for as long as the church has been in existence*" [109] —that is *really not true*. The leaders of the Emerging Church are obviously willing to lead us back to the *Middle Ages,* the days of the *medieval* church at Rome—but *NOT* to the Early Church, the *apostolic* church in the days of Christ and His apostles, *who would not compromise Truth even at the threat of death!*

"JOIN THE CONVERSATION!"

Combining a recognition of people's tendency to chat and "schmooze" with its own aversion to Bible preaching, the Emerging Church conducts most of its services as "a **conversation**." It works like this: A fellow sits on a bar stool before the congregation (who are mostly in their twenties), lounging in a semicircle. But rather than giving a sermon, he asks questions, suggesting several options for answers, and often joins the conversation himself.

Roger Oakland, a Christian author who has followed the Emerging Church movement since its inception, makes this evaluation:

With obscure language, a seemingly noble cause, and evasive [and often aimless] *conversations,* the Emerging Church is mesmerizing many people (including Christians), receiving the support of established Christian leaders, and leaving a trail of **confusion** and **disarray** in its path. [110]

Thus the Emerging Church offers *NOT* **Bible doctrine** *but* **babbling dialogue,** *NOT* **salvation** but **searching.** "In a sense, *always searching but never finding* is a trademark of the Emerging Church, because in the endless dialogue (*conversation*), the Truth is never found." [111] That's because, having *rudely shoved aside* God's revelations in Scripture, those misguided seekers are—in the words of Paul—"ever learning, and never able to come to the knowledge of the Truth." [112]

Five hundred years ago the Protestant Reformation corrected many errors that had crept into the church. As a reaction against erroneous *manmade* teachings, the Reformers' battle-cry was "*Sola Scriptura*"—Scripture alone! That inspired rule has served us well whenever it's been followed. But now the Emerging Church gurus tell us we need "a **New** Reformation."

So we must ask those "spiritual leaders"—Please tell us again: *Why is it* that we supposedly need this Emerging Church **rebellion** against *Sola Scriptura? And why* is the slogan now *not* "Scripture alone" but *"Anything BUT Scripture"?*

MULTI-SENSORY WORSHIP

SIGHT: Although flames from several candles dance on the walls, lighting is minimal and very subdued. But this is what leaders of the Emerging Church recommend. Dan Kimball gives us at least his personal assurance:

> In the emerging culture, **DARKNESS represents spirituality**. We see this in Buddhist temples, as well as Catholic and Orthodox churches. **Darkness** communicates that *something SERIOUS is happening.* [113]

Imagine that! Kimball says that *"darkness represents spirituality."* That's what I would call *"spiritual darkness"!*

SMELL: The fragrance of incense fills the corners of the room.

One article titled "Ancient New" tries to back up the idea that postmoderns are looking for a sensual, experiential worship:

> Post-moderns prefer to encounter Christ by **using ALL their SENSES.** That's part of the appeal of classical liturgical or **contemplative worship:** *the incense and candles, making the sign of the cross, the taste and smell of the bread and wine, touching icons, and being anointed with oil.* [114]

But Christian author Roger Oakland, in his excellent exposé of the Emerging Church, raises this caution:

> While the Emerging Church and many Christian authors promote the view that ***mystical encounters*** and ***sensory engagements*** are a more effective tool for evangelism, they are **NOT** supported by Scripture. However, those ideas **CAN** be found in ***church tradition*** as Chuck Fromm comments in his article:
>
> > "In many ways, the Church is *seeking a way back* to its oldest and most sacred traditions: those in which **ALL the SENSES are fully engaged** in the act of worship—from ***incense*** and ***bells*** to ***icons*** and ***vestments***." [115]

Yet not everyone finds all those non-Scriptural "trimmings" attractive. Dan Kimball quotes an older gentleman who expressed serious concerns about the many radical changes in his worship service:

> Dan, *why did you use* **INCENSE**? *[Not all incense smells pleasantly fragrant. Some varieties just downright smell!]* I am not sure I like walking over to those "**prayer stations**" with all those props; *can't we just pray from our seats? Why aren't you just* **PREACHING from the Bible?** I wasn't too comfortable when you had those **times of SILENCE**, and it's a little **TOO DARK** in there for me. [116]

3. Brian McLaren 1956–

This movement is called the "Emerging" or "Emergent" Church, and one of its main leaders, Brian McLaren, has grown tired of the Christian church. He wants to *deconstruct* the old and *reconstruct* a new kind of Christian faith. The titles of two of his books, *Everything Must Change* and *A New Kind of Christianity,* reflect his desires, echoing the Emerging Church movement's interest in **RADICAL** theological reformulation and its focus on new ways of "doing church" and expressing our spirituality. Here he lets us know that "new" is his favorite word:

> If we have a new world, we will need *a new church*. We won't need a new religion *per se* [that is, *in itself*], but *a new framework for our theology*. Not a new Spirit, but *a new spirituality*. Not a new Christ, but *a new Christian*. Not a new denomination, but *a new kind of church in every denomination.* [117]

But King Solomon, blessed by God as the wisest man who ever lived, flatly contradicts those plans in these inspired words: *"There is nothing new under the sun."* —**Ecclesiastes 1:9.** See also **1 Kings 3:5–28.**

McLaren's ideas are not based on the Bible. Not only are they not found in the Bible, but they won't work with an intact Bible. In order for the

Emerging Church to succeed, the Bible must be looked at through entirely different glasses, and Christianity needs to be open to a new type of faith. McLaren calls this new faith "a *generous* orthodoxy"—which is also the title of another of his books.[118] Such an orthodoxy allows *a smorgasbord of ideas* to be proclaimed in the name of Christ, many of which are actually forbidden and rejected by Scripture.[119]

Phyllis Tickle, a best-selling author and the founding editor of the religion department at *Publishers Weekly,* is also a friend of the Emerging Church. In her book *The Great Emergence* she asserts that "Brian McLaren is to this new reformation [of the Emerging Church] what Martin Luther was to the Protestant Reformation."[120] The first chapter in that book she calls *Rummage Sales: When the Church Cleans Out Its Attic* and quotes Anglican bishop Mark Dyer as saying that

> about every five hundred years, the Church feels compelled to hold a *giant rummage sale.* And . . . we are living in and through one of those five-hundred-year sales. . . . Every five hundred years, the empowered structures of institutionalized Christianity, **WHATEVER** *they may be*, . . . *must be* **SHATTERED** so that renewal and growth may occur.[121]

Devout Bible believers may well fear that to Emergent leaders the above words "whatever they may be" include bedrock Scriptural truth and teaching. But I appreciate McLaren's candidness when he admitted it isn't just the way the message is presented that Emerging Church proponents want to change —it's the message itself they're changing:

> It has been fashionable among the innovative [Emergent] pastors I know to say, "We're *NOT* changing the *message;* we're only changing the *medium.*" This claim is probably <u>less than honest</u> . . . in the new church we must realize how *medium and message are intertwined.* When we change the medium, the message that's received is changed, however subtly, as well. We might as well get beyond our naïveté or denial about this.[122]

The Emerging Church has *sold out Christianity* by using high-tech marketing methods to create their "seeker friendly" congregations with a watered-down gospel—one that de-emphasizes sin and repentance and promotes sensual approaches to a counterfeit "worship."

Thus we see all too clearly that Emerging Church leaders like Dan Kimball, Robert Webber, and Brian McLaren desperately pretend to offer fashionably new ideas on the cutting-edge of the future (with some major compromises thrown in for good measure). But in reality—for all their fancy terminology of Ancient-Future, Emerging, Vintage, and so forth—the only thing they have to peddle is <u>Satan's same OLD poison packaged in NEW bottles!</u>

PART III.
DEADLY DANGERS OF CONTEMPLATIVE PRAYER

Before dealing with the vulnerability of innocent believers being dangerously exposed to the direct influence of Satan's devils, let me take a moment to highlight *one factor that must not be overlooked.*

A. YOUR VOLUNTARY *CONSENT* IS REQUIRED

Montenegro, in her careful and illuminating first-person report on the lecture by Catholic monk and abbot Thomas Keating, mentioned one thing that really caught my attention. She said Keating told students of his Centering Prayer session that we must "consent" to the present moment. She particularly noticed his word *consent*—and stated in her report—"This word was used a lot." [123]

The reason that this was an important—and repeated—part of his lesson is that *God gave all mankind the divine gift of **FREE WILL**.* Every man and woman is a free moral agent. Now, some Christians foolishly presume that "'*The Silence*' poses **NO** *spiritual danger—and if it **DID**, God would **PROTECT** us in it!*"

But they are dead wrong to be so presumptuous, because God has **already TOLD us**—very strongly in His Word—to have **NOTHING** to do with spirits or spiritualism. Yet, if we *choose* to exercise His gift of FREE CHOICE and dabble in the dangers of mysticism against His will, God won't stop us. In fact, He **CAN'T** stop us and protect us when we deliberately, willfully put ourselves on the devil's ground. To do that would mean CHANGING the way He CREATED us.

It must have hurt God terribly to watch Eve—and then Adam—as they started to hang around the mysterious Tree of Knowledge of Good and Evil. He foresaw the danger and wanted to protect them, but in the great love He felt for them, He had already clearly warned them. So recognizing their great gift of Free Choice, He didn't *stop* them from disobeying and sinning—and He couldn't intervene and *protect* them from the Serpent, Satan. For without Free Will and Freedom of Choice, mankind would be mere robots or puppets pulled by invisible strings.

By the same token, we can be sure it's painful for our loving Lord to watch His children expose themselves—by their own foolish *choice* and "consent" to the whispered lies and false teachings of "silver-tongued devils." But God **WILL NOT** overrule our free choice or "bulldoze" our free will by bullying us to obey Him. Therefore, when we willfully and deliberately choose to disobey Him, He **CANNOT** protect us from the consequences of our choice.

The Prodigal Son's father [124] wasn't able to keep him from making a foolish decision, but when he came to his senses, his father welcomed him back. And so will our kind heavenly Father—yet in His wisdom He knows that though our wounds may heal, scars sometimes remain.

The *consent* of our free will is almost always required in the case of sin or of habits that are bad for us. Smoking is not at first an addiction or even a pleasant thing to do. Kids who secretly try it may cough and even feel sick. One has to work at it to get used to it. The same with alcohol, for whiskey and other liquors taste like *bad medicine* to most youngsters—not pleasantly sweet like pure grape juice.

It seems that God has arranged "the rules of the game" so that the devil cannot **FORCE** us to sin. From Adam on down to the last one on earth, we must **consent** to it. So that's what the demons are waiting for, quite patiently, in the darkness of "the Silence": They **know** *we must be willing, we must consent.* This invisible factor is seen even in a court of law: In a case of INVOLUNTARY MANSLAUGHTER the victim is every bit as *dead* as in a case of PREMEDITATED MURDER IN THE FIRST DEGREE—but the penalty for the latter charge is much greater.

God doesn't want us ever to consent to such a crime. And He has told us never to consent to the mystic meditation of New Age spiritualism. Now, as we proceed to examine the very real dangers of Contemplative Prayer, let's be comforted by the knowledge that we'll be SAFE as long as we never CONSENT to take part in it.

B. Perilous Exposure to Demonic Influence

In our section above on "the Silence," we saw how those supposedly "praying" are exposed in that mystical experience to trances and self-hypnotism! Those things are indeed *bad enough*—few people would subject themselves to *such a loss of control* if they knew in advance what was involved.

But a *much more SERIOUS threat* is the danger of being exposed to **DIRECT CONTACT** with evil spirits called *demons and devils!* Lest we mistakenly think this sounds like something out of a fictional horror story, the apostle Paul, writing under Inspiration, soberly declares:

> We wrestle **NOT** against flesh and blood, but against principalities, against **POWERS**, against the **RULERS of the DARKNESS** of this world, against **SPIRITUAL WICKEDNESS** in high places. —**Ephesians 6:12**, KJV.

And Christian writer and researcher Ray Yungen hauls scoffers back to reality with these wise words:

> As Christians, we often **forget** that familiar spirits are *fallen angels,* once created to minister as messengers and worshipping spirits for

God. They *know how* to sound spiritually positive, and they *know how* to communicate God's truths [*—OR Satan's LIES!*] [125]

Yungen goes on to tell how Dr. Rodney R. Romney, former senior pastor of the First Baptist Church of Seattle—a person frequently quoted as an example of "a New Age Christian"—*very candidly revealed* what was conveyed to him in his Contemplative Prayer periods. He said the "source of wisdom" he was in contact with told him the following:

> I want you to preach this **oneness**, to hold it up before the world as my call to **unity** and **togetherness**. In the end this witness to the **oneness of ALL** people will undermine any barriers that presently exist. [126]

Could this be the voice of a demon? Jesus Christ *never* taught that all people are one. There are the *saved* and the *unsaved*, or to put it figuratively, "the *sheep* and the *goats*." And Jesus Himself explicitly made this distinction, as the whole Bible does on a number of occasions. [127]

But the spirit who spoke to Dr. Romney *also* revealed something else of VITAL importance. It declared, "*SILENCE is that place, that environment where I work.*" [128] And Yungen urges:

> *Please pay attention to this!* God does **NOT** work in the silence[129] —but familiar spirits **DO**. Moreover, *what makes it so dangerous* is that *they are very clever*. One well-known New Ager revealed what his guiding (familiar) spirit candidly disclosed: [130] "We [spirits] work with all who are vibrationally sympathetic; [131] simple and sincere people who feel our spirit moving, *but for the most part, only **WITHIN** the context of their current belief system*." [132]

Those last quoted words are from an unearthly spirit—one of the spirits Ray Yungen says "are very clever." Do you see *HOW* they prove themselves to be fiendishly clever? Just as a fisherman patiently "plays" a fish until he's sure it has taken the bait and the hook is firmly implanted, the demons from Satan's legions are careful **NOT** to say anything that might go against the Christian's "*current* belief system." Those "current" beliefs may *change radically AFTER* a time of hearing "wonderful" new concepts, beautifully novel doctrines that are 180 degrees removed from the Christian beliefs and teachings with which one began! We mustn't scare the quarry away—right?

So Satan, who has had at least six thousand years to make an in-depth study of the human mind—plenty of time to become the most brilliant psychologist in the world—uses all his craft and cunning to teach his demon lackeys just *what* to say and *how* to say it.

A Pleasant Mind-Body "Experience"

And because *there's so much at stake*—after all, the demons' very survival depends on their success, [133] so *they're playing this "game" for keeps!*—you can be sure they make their contemplative deception as absolutely *enticing* and *alluring* as possible. One authority is Ken Kaisch, an Episcopal priest and teacher himself of mystical prayer, who says this in his book *Finding God: A Handbook of Christian Meditation:*

> You will gradually be able to tune into God's <u>Presence</u> . . . you will have *a sense of slow, vibrant, deep energy* surrounding you. . . . Let yourself flow with this energy, it is the <u>Presence</u> of our Lord. . . . As you *continue* to dwell in this <u>Presence</u>, *the INTENSITY will GROW. It is EXTREMELY PLEASURABLE to <u>experience</u>.* [134]

That word, *experience,* is a word *often* used in Spiritual Formation circles. Listen to what Leonard Sweet, a leader in the movement, says:

> <u>Mysticism</u>, *once cast to the SIDELINES* of the Christian tradition, is *NOW* situated in post-modern culture *near the CENTER.* . . . In the words of one of the greatest theologians of the twentieth century, Jesuit philosopher of religion Karl Rahner, "The Christian of tomorrow will be a <u>mystic</u>, one who has **EXPERIENCED** something, or he will be nothing." [<u>Mysticism</u>] is metaphysics arrived at through mind-body **EXPERIENCES**. <u>Mysticism</u> *begins* in **EXPERIENCE**; it *ends* in theology. [135]

(This means, incidentally, that mystics ***don't like*** theology; they ***hate*** doctrine, and they ***despise*** the Bible. But ***oooh!*** they *LOVE* "experiences!")

Many agree that this feeling—this "experience"—is quite "pleasurable," though some use other words—like *ecstasy,* as does Calvin Miller, a Baptist mystic whose book *Into the Depths of God* is brimming with quotes from Thomas Merton and other promoters of Contemplative Prayer. Miller speaks of the "wonderful relationship between *ECSTASY* [the mystical state] and transcendence [God]," and says that "**ecstasy** is meant to increase our desire for heaven." [136] This state of "**Ecstasy**" is the same state that Thomas Merton *likened to an LSD trip* and which made him say he wanted to be *the best Buddhist he could be!* [137]

Reports like these—about "pleasurable" feelings of "ecstasy" and such —help us understand *WHY* many formerly staunch and steadfast Christians seem willing to compromise their beliefs and become more liberal and lukewarm. When people have this "experience," they *like* it and *want* it to continue. People once hooked on an addiction—whether it's gambling, drugs, or even mysticism—find that it "grows" on them. They like it more and more and refuse even to listen to reasonable arguments about how they're hurting themselves. The demons, of course, understand all this and are glad that it works in their favor.

But still, experience is "not all it's cracked up to be." The mystics like

Leonard Sweet can say what they want to, they can tell us how important and wonderful they think experience is. But what they DON'T tell us is that to expect God to give us an *"EXPERIENCE"* is to **deny** our faith. **Hebrews 11:1** gives a beautiful definition of true "faith" as "the **substance** of *things hoped for,* the **evidence** of *things not seen."* That's the kind of faith God wants us to have—**even now**, *before* we get to heaven, *before* we see Him face to face— rock-solid faith even in things *NOT* experienced, in "things *NOT [yet] seen"*!

Faith—like hope, love, truth, justice—is an intangible abstraction: you can't touch it or weigh it on a scale, saying, "I have two pounds of faith here!" All those abstract concepts are very real, precious things—yet imperceptible to our senses unless and until they manifest themselves in some way. Our definition also says, "Faith is the **substance** of things *hoped for."* And in **Romans 8:24** God had Paul explain *hope* in a way similar to that of *faith:* "Hope that is SEEN is NOT hope; for why does one still hope for what he sees?"

So if we really demand a *mystical*—that is, a direct, personal, firsthand— **"experience"** from God to let you *see, hear, touch* Him in His "Presence," then **we are refusing to accept the evidence** already given in the Bible. The disciple called "Doubting Thomas" was just such a skeptic, saying he would not believe Jesus was resurrected unless he could not only SEE the risen Christ but also TOUCH Him, putting his finger into the nail holes in His hands, and his hand into the spear-wound in His side!

When Jesus came, He kindly indulged Thomas's request and invited him to touch Him. But please note carefully Christ's next words, words that show that believers who have **FAITH** do not—and *should not*—NEED an experience like that of Thomas's:

> Jesus said to him, "Thomas, because you have SEEN Me, you have believed. **Blessed are those who have NOT seen and yet have believed."** [138]

When I recall that God teaches that we are SAVED by grace through "FAITH"—**Ephesians 2:8**—and that "FAITH" is the VICTORY—**1 John 5:4**—it makes me think that those promoters of "experience" are like a pack of hounds out for the hunt, who are "barking up the WRONG tree." For in so doing they leave FAITH out of the equation completely!

So Christian believers don't call upon God to give them *personal demonstrations* or *mystic experiences* to strengthen their faith—and the Bible does not lead us to expect that. But notice the mystical, out-of-body "experience" Richard Foster recommends in *Celebration of Discipline:*

> In your *imagination* allow your spiritual body, shining with light, to *rise out of your physical body. . . . Reassure your body that you will return.*

. . . Go deeper and deeper into outer space until there is nothing except the warm *presence* of the eternal Creator. Rest in his *presence. Listen quietly . . . [to] any instruction given.* [139]

This is undisguised *astral projection* and *occult contact* through the *imagination* and is the major technique used by *shamans* and *medicine men* acting as *MEDIUMS* to contact their spirit guides! Yet Foster claims—and wants us to believe—that it leads to Christ and God:

Take a single event [from Scripture]. Seek to LIVE the experience, remembering the encouragement of **Ignatius of Loyola** [the Catholic mystic and founder of the Jesuits] to *apply all our senses* to our task. . . . Enter the story, not as a passive observer but as an active participant. . . . *You can ACTUALLY encounter the LIVING Christ in the event, be addressed by His voice and be touched by His healing power. . . . Jesus Christ will ACTUALLY come to you.* [140]

ACTUALLY this teaching is not true! You **cannot** call the real Jesus Christ from the right hand of the Father to appear to you—*but any **DEMON** will be happy to **pretend** to be "Jesus"!*

In the "Golden Age of Radio" everyone heard the announcer's voice resonating with the same words each time before the President spoke: ***"The next voice you hear*** will be that of the **President** of the United States." Then FDR would begin by saying, "My friends, . . ."

But—as you travel down this mystically silent path of Contemplative Prayer, ***the next voice you hear*** may **NOT** be that of God but of "**the god of this world**"—as Paul refers to Satan in **2 Corinthians 4:4**, KJV.

1. EVEN PRACTITIONERS AND PROPONENTS *ADMIT ITS DANGERS!*

Before considering the sober warnings of promoters and teachers of Contemplative Prayer, let me share the insights of a *former* practitioner. Pastor Rick Howard recently completed thirty-three years as a minister of the gospel in the eastern and central United States. But before his conversion to Christ, he spent five years in the supernatural arena of the New Age, learning secrets of the occult and experiencing firsthand its mystical madness. But after being chillingly frightened during a séance, he turned his back on all that, and the Lord led him into a close servant relationship with the King of kings. His unique experiences in both the New Age and Christianity provide an insider's view, which he shares in his book *The Omega Rebellion* (2010). The ideas on the next page and a half are predominantly his, though in a few cases paraphrased instead of quoted directly.

From the most ancient times, and throughout *ALL* the occult and mystical literature, there runs a common teaching:

1. *that trained practitioners of <u>meditative techniques</u>*
2. *can reach an <u>altered state of consciousness</u> that enables them*
3. *to <u>contact directly</u> the world of the <u>supernatural</u>.*

And this teaching—far from being "make believe"—is actually TRUE. *We CAN indeed contact the supernatural!* But please *remember* . . . ever since Lucifer's rebellion in heaven the "supernatural" world has included BOTH Good *and Evil,* BOTH Angels *and Demons!*

It is essential to learn these *mystical meditative techniques of mind control* to get to that certain mental level where one is able to contact and communicate directly with supernatural beings. This unique corridor of the mind can be reached only through certain meditative practices that *always involve a <u>focusing of the mind</u> to the exclusion of anything else—a quieting and silencing of the mind.*

When a person enters this "Silence" he's entering a place where *the powers of evil angels can create any illusion they desire.* For example:

1. **A person practicing Hinduism** may experience during this demonically controlled moment a vision of his favorite guru levitating over the river Ganges.

2. **A spirit medium/channeler** will believe he's in contact with the spirit of a dead person, when he's really communicating with a fallen angel, a demon impersonating the one who passed away.

3. **A psychic "mind reader"** enters that corridor of the mind when reading the mind of a subject. He will be given a thought by the demon, who gives *the same thought* to the one whose mind is supposedly being read. When the psychic reveals the thought, it appears as if he has read the mind of the subject, when in reality the thought was injected into **both** their minds by a fallen angel.

4. And finally, **the modern-day Christian,** upon entering **"the Silence,"** will believe he has come into the direct presence of God, <u>when in reality he is under the control of the **SAME** demonic powers</u> as the psychics, spirit mediums, and ancient mystics of the church—those of *any* religion or pagan group that relies on <u>mystical</u>, <u>supernatural</u> EXPERIENCES as evidence of their contact with God.

This is the power Satan has over people who use these meditative techniques, even if they are used unknowingly and are deceived, believing there's nothing wrong with their use. **Exactly the SAME methods have been used for thousands of years** and are the secrets behind *EVERY* mystical experience, whether by early mystics of the Christian church like the Desert Fathers or a thousand years earlier, by Hindu masters. It's **always the SAME**—this entering into **"the Silence"** is <u>necessary</u> for the supernatural experience.

We must realize that WE do not control _the time_ when God communicates with us. HE does. If we believe God is at our beck and call by entering an altered state through the use of meditative or prayer techniques, we deceive ourselves and commit the sin of presumption. Even more dangerous is the fact that we are communicating with demons and are practicing spiritualism, _which God—knowing the perils thereof—condemns in the strongest possible terms to protect us!_ [141]

***   ***   ***

I appreciate Pastor Howard's frank and helpful explanation from _someone who's "been there, done that."_ Personally, I fervently believe what I've been saying here about the danger—the very **_REAL_** danger—of "the Silence" of Contemplative Prayer opening us up to evil spirits, those invisible supernatural beings who loathe us—_and God_—with a venomous hatred. I'm convinced of this danger in my own mind—because the Bible tells me so. [142]

But readers need not take **my word** for it. Many promoters of Contemplative Prayer **_themselves_** recognize its genuine potential dangers! Let's see what Richard Foster says as a prime mover in the early days of this movement and the one person more responsible than any other for popularizing it. Remarkably enough, Foster himself gives us this caution:

> So that we may not be led astray, however, we _MUST_ understand that we are _NOT_ engaging in some flippant work. We are not calling on some cosmic bellhop. _It is **serious and even DANGEROUS** business._ [143]

And the German Benedictine monk—and master of Zen Buddhism— Willigis Jager, himself a promoter of mystic meditation, forthrightly admits:

> Christian literature makes reference to _many episodes_ that parallel the experiences of those going the _yogic_ way [that is, the mystic way of Hinduism's yoga]. Saint Anthony, one of the first desert mystics, _FREQUENTLY encountered STRANGE and sometimes TERRIFYING psychophysical forces_ while at prayer. [144]

In response to these admissions about mystical prayer being "dangerous business" and "terrifying" people, as well as other similar cautions, Christian author Roger Oakland in his book, _Faith Undone_ asks: "What is this—praying to _the God of the Bible_ but instead reaching _demons?_ Maybe _Contemplative Prayer_ should be renamed _Contemplative Terror._" [145]

Even David Hazard, the editor of the NAVPRESS Spiritual Formation line of books (Spiritual Formation books _promote_ Contemplative Prayer), honestly admits: **"Not all** the 'spiritualities' and 'spiritual practices' offered to us today **are biblical, _or safe._"** [146]

And, to his credit, the author of that same book Hazard edited, Dr. Bruce

Demarest, professor at Denver Seminary, candidly confesses:

> I also have serious concerns. *Spirituality* is a buzzword in our culture, covering the waterfront from African voodoo to Zen Buddhist practices [that is, from **A** to **Z**]. ***Not everything*** *that stirs the soul* ***is from God.*** . . . We are bombarded with *exotic* [foreign] spiritual practices, such as *yoga* and forms of *meditations* that supposedly lead a person back through past lives. [147]

I mentioned before the Desert Fathers being hermits, ascetics, monks, and nuns (Desert Mothers) who lived mainly in the Egyptian desert near Alexandria beginning around the third century A.D. One rather ironic excerpt from *The Sayings of the Desert Fathers* declares:

> A hermit said, "Take care to be **silent. Empty** your mind. Attend to your meditation in the fear of God, whether you are resting or at work. If you do this, you will not fear the attacks of the **demons**." [148]

Starting with *Celebration of Discipline* in 1978, Richard Foster urged that we "should ALL without shame enroll as apprentices in the school of Contemplative Prayer." [149] *And yet,* in his later book (1992), *Prayer: Finding the Heart's True Home,* Foster gives a word of WARNING and PRECAUTION that this is a ***dangerous prayer method*** that can invoke **DEMONIC** activity and requires special protection:

> At the outset I need to give **a word of WARNING.** . . . Contemplative Prayer is *NOT* for the *NOVICE.* I do not say this about any other form of prayer. . . . Contemplative prayer is for *those who have exercised their spiritual muscles* a bit and know something about the landscape of the *spirit.* In fact, those who work in the area of *spiritual direction* **always** look for signs of a **maturing** faith **before** encouraging individuals into Contemplative Prayer. . . .
>
> I also want to give **a word of PRECAUTION.** In the silent contemplation of God we are entering *deeply* into the spiritual realm, and there *IS* such a thing as a ***supernatural*** guidance that is *NOT divine* guidance. While the Bible *does not give us a lot of information* on the nature of the spiritual world [not true!], we do know . . . ***there are various orders of spiritual beings, and some of them are DEFINITELY NOT in cooperation with God and His way!*** . . . But for now I want to encourage you to ***LEARN and PRACTICE*** *prayers of* ***PROTECTION.*** . . . "**All dark and evil spirits must now leave.**" [150]

Such a notion is hard for former New Agers to understand. Of Foster's incongruous **warning,** one former New Ager asks:

> **Why would God ASK us to become involved in a type of prayer that could bring exposure to and harm from DEMONIC**

influences? Foster warns that *a novice Christian should not engage in it. . . .* Why would Foster or **any** believer **WANT** to practice such a form of prayer? Could it be they are infatuated with the seductive feeling that accompanies it—and like other contemplatives, feel the need to get closer to God? But . . . it is the finished work of Christ on the Cross that allows us access to the throne of God, and that access is immediately available to us the moment we're born-again. It's not just for an elite group of people "mature" enough to handle it; no, it is for all who have been born of the Spirit and justified by faith. [151]

Obviously, anyone who puts himself or herself in harm's way by indulging in Contemplative Prayer should *pray for protection,* as even the leaders of the movement themselves advise. But let's keep two things in mind:

1. Is it not the height of *PRESUMPTION* on one's part to pray to the Lord, "God, I've decided to go now into the dark Silence where the evil spirits are waiting—where you've warned me *NOT* to go. But please *protect me and keep me safe!"*

2. *Nowhere* in the Bible are we required or told to pray a prayer of "protection" *before we PRAY!!!*

So, in light of those two points, we may be excused if we wonder aloud whether Richard Foster knows **"What's WRONG with this Picture?"**

2. THE AWFUL "ALPHA" OF MIND CONTROL!

Mike Perschon, a freelance writer for Youth Specialties,[152] wrote of his own exploration of the mystical life:

> I started using the phrase "listening prayer" when I talked about my own experiences in meditation. I built myself a prayer room—a tiny sanctuary in a basement closet filled with books on spiritual disciplines, contemplative prayer, and Christian mysticism. In that space I lit candles, burned incense, hung rosaries, and listened to tapes of Benedictine monks. I meditated for hours on words, images, and sounds. I reached the point of being able to achieve *alpha brain patterns,* the state in which dreams occur, while still awake and meditating. [153]

Christian writer Ray Yungen reacts in these words:

When I hear a Christian talking like this, it creates a very deep concern within me for that person *because I know what is meant by "alpha."* [154]

And he shares some of this as follows:

Throughout Laurie Cabot's book, *Power of the Witch,* **alpha** is a term she uses to mean *meditation* or *"the Silence."* In fact, she makes no secret of it but confides:

The science of Witchcraft is **based** on our ability to enter an altered state of consciousness we call "**alpha**." In **alpha** *the mind opens up* to **non-ordinary** forms of communication, such as telepathy, clairvoyance, and precognition. Here we also may . . . *receive mystical visionary information* that does *NOT* come through the five senses. In **alpha** the rational FILTERS that process ordinary reality are *weakened* or *removed*, and *the mind is RECEPTIVE* to **non-ordinary realities**. [155]

Yungen says *the absolute importance* of this practice is made clear throughout Cabot's book. Without it, there is no "power." She explains:

Alpha is the *springboard* for **ALL** psychic and magical workings. It is the **heart** of Witchcraft. . . . You **must** master it **first** before proceeding to any other spell, ritual, or exercise in this book. . . .

Mystics in EVERY religious tradition speak of **alpha** states of consciousness and the lure of Divine Light, although they do so in their own metaphors and images. In their own ways they have learned how to enter **alpha** as they pray or worship. They have learned how to become *[supposedly]* enlightened. [156]

Yet our all-knowing God was fully aware that this would happen—that people would be enamored and seduced by false teachings. And He inspired Paul to write this explicit, prophetic warning to those who would heed it:

Now the Spirit speaketh expressly, that *in the latter times* some shall *depart from the faith*, giving heed to **SEDUCING SPIRITS**, and **DOCTRINES of DEVILS**. [157]

Hindus, Buddhists, and other pagan mystics have been happy in their seduction to ecstatic trances and the whispering of spirits *for many centuries*. This prediction contained in Paul's scripture above is not referring to them—that would certainly be "Old News." No, God is saying here that CHRISTIANS, those who were taught the true way of Christ's salvation, would "*depart* from the faith, giving heed to *seducing spirits*." And **WHEN** would this tragedy occur? "In the latter days"—shortly before our Lord returns!

Sadly enough, we see that prophecy being fulfilled before our very eyes. Our all-wise God surely knows the *END* from the *BEGINNING*.

+ + +

C. Undermining the Authority of God's Word

We've considered the teachings and opinions of many advocates for Contemplative Prayer in these pages. But perhaps we should ask ourselves, "What kind of men are they? Are they the kind who respect the Word of

God, who have a high regard for the Bible?" That's often a good barometer of a Christian's "spirituality"—to use one of their own favorite words.

1. *Deliberately Misquoting Scripture*

Do the teachers and spiritual leaders of Contemplative Prayer **take liberties** with the Bible and **misquote** important Scriptures? Yes, they do. Let's look at some examples.

✓ **Example Number One** is seen when Thomas Keating—the *founder* of Centering Prayer—misquotes Jesus Himself as saying in **Mark 8:34**, "Unless you deny your inmost self and take up the cross, you cannot be My disciple." He adds a word (*inmost*) that is *not there*. Then he says, "Denial of our inmost self includes detachment from the habitual functioning of our intellect and will, which are our inmost faculties." [158]

Now any of us can make an honest mistake, and we should be quick to understand and forgive our fellows' human errors. But in this case, to put it plainly, it seems that Keating *smuggled in* this word *purposely*—with a *deliberate* design to help his cause. Here's why it seems that way:

A. Keating first *chooses* a word specifically needed for his teaching.

B. Then he *inserts* it into God's holy Scripture—*among Christ's own quoted words.*

C. Next, in his own sentence, added for interpretive purposes, he *again inserts* his chosen word—*TWICE, for good measure!*

Thus Keating succeeds in planting—*three times*—an *illegitimate* thought into the "inmost faculties" of his readers who would never suspect him of using underhanded methods to teach "God's Truth."

But we must understand that teachers of Contemplative Prayer *must feel frustrated* because the inspired Word of God offers them NO support, neither here in this verse nor elsewhere. For the meaning of this scripture text is to carry our crosses and deny ourselves. *It has **NOTHING** to do with mind-emptying.*

✓ **Example Number Two** is seen when Keating *adds two whole sentences of completely new thoughts* to **Luke 10:20** when **he quotes the Lord Jesus** as saying,

> Do not get excited about that kind of success. Anybody can work miracles with a little psychic energy and the divine assistance. What you should rejoice over is that your names are written in heaven. [159]

Those first two sentences do not exist. And Jesus would never suggest the use of "psychic energy." Here again Keating takes liberties with God's Word and dares to incorporate *his own* misleading ideas into it!

We've just seen that Keating doesn't mind misquoting Scripture in general or even Jesus in particular. But note that he is a rather prominent Roman Catholic member of the clergy—as are *many other* Contemplative Prayer proponents, as you may have noticed, such as Merton, Nouwen, Pennington, and many others. And my research reveals that in teaching this mystical technique of prayer, they are *out of harmony* not only with the Bible but also with official Catholic authorities. So I'll count this as . . .

✓ **Example Number Three:** Though this is not misquoting *the Bible*, it **IS** a case of Catholic mystics <u>going against</u> what they pretend to respect as spiritual authority which in their mind is *as high as* the Bible.

For instance, throughout their books on Contemplative Prayer, Catholic monks Keating and Pennington repeatedly mention **St. Teresa of Avila** (1515–1582), implying that she was an advocate of their prayer techniques. However, in reading her books we find that *her teachings on prayer are the* **OPPOSITE** of what Keating and Pennington are teaching.

First of all, she says that *contemplation is a GIFT from God,* and *NO TECHNIQUE can make it happen.* She says it is usually given to people who have a deep prayer life and are practicing many virtues, though God can give it to anyone He chooses. She repeatedly insists that contemplation is *DIVINELY produced.* She said that entering into the prayer of **quiet** or that of **union** *whenever she wanted it* **"was OUT of the question."** [160]

She also said in her book, *Interior Mansion,* "For it to **BE** prayer at all, *the MIND MUST take part in it.*" [161] Both of the above-quoted statements are not only crystal clear, they are also diametrically opposed to what we hear from Catholic teachers of Contemplative Prayer!

And in 1989, Cardinal Ratzinger, before becoming Pope Benedict XVI, wrote a booklet to the worldwide church *cautioning against* certain forms of meditation or prayer—especially the practice of encouraging believers to *empty their minds.* In this booklet Ratzinger quotes the pope on that subject:

> Pope John Paul II has pointed out to the whole Church the example and doctrine of St. Teresa of Avila who in her life had to **REJECT** *the temptation of certain methods.* . . . In a homily [that is, a sermon] given on November 1, 1982, he [the Pope] . . . [spoke] "*<u>AGAINST some methods of prayer</u> which are <u>NOT inspired by the gospel</u> and which in practice tend to set Christ aside <u>in preference for a **MENTAL VOID**</u> which **MAKES NO SENSE** in Christianity.*" [162]

Finally, in the teaching manual of the Roman Catholic Church—the latest edition of their official *Catechism*—we read under the heading of

"OBJECTIONS TO PRAYER," that "We must face in ourselves and around us *erroneous* notions of prayer. Some people view prayer as . . . an effort of concentration to reach a MENTAL VOID." [163]

How those many Roman Catholic voices and pens can so enthusiastically promote a mystical method of prayer which is *officially condemned* by their own church, I shall leave for them to explain to us.

✓ **Example Number Four is again a bit different—but by no means unique in today's world.** Ex-priest of the Roman Catholic Church Brennan Manning can hardly be accused of misquoting the Bible—for the simple reason that he rarely uses Scripture in his books or in his public meetings. But what he *does* do is just as bad, or perhaps worse: He presents himself as an authoritative teacher of God's Truth and then *gives his OWN ideas with NO reference to Scripture!*

Look: A major theme of Manning's *The Ragamuffin Gospel* is "trusting the love of God," because God loves you no matter what you do. There is *NO* call to sanctification or holiness. Instead, Manning excuses sin as a human weakness that God will tolerate—*regardless* of whether the sinner is *repentant or not.* In teaching this, Manning has joined the ranks of "ungodly persons who turn the *grace* of our God into *licentiousness*"—**Jude 4**, NASB.

Instead of teaching people what the Bible says, Brennan Manning much prefers to share his own ideas and opinions.

For example, in his books *The Signature of God* and *Gentle Revolutionaries* Manning describes a dream he has had about Judgment Day. He sees Adolf Hitler and Hugh Hefner (founder of *Playboy* magazine) and himself and others going before God to be judged. But God just takes them by the hand and walks them home! The implication is that *everyone* is accepted by God through grace, *regardless* of whether they repent and believe the gospel and have a born-again experience. Manning even claims that those who take the Mark of the Beast will be saved! Please note:

And He [Christ] will say to us: "Vile beings, you who are in the image of the beast and bear his mark, but come all the same, you as well." [164]

Taking liberties with the Bible is putting it mildly! Manning "misquotes" it so horribly he seems to be "making up" God's Word as he goes along.

2. *DOWNGRADING AND DENIGRATING THE BIBLE*

Mystical experience becomes a problem—and a deadly danger—when it becomes *a source of revelation, a private avenue of insight into God and His workings.* It thereby undermines the believer's commitment to Scripture as the sole source of revelation. The Scriptures nowhere teach that God gives us any knowledge through supposed "spiritual experience" but, on the contrary, they damn and curse those who unwisely dabble in spiritualism.

True knowledge of spiritual matters is always linked to God's revelation, the written Word. So mysticism is simply not an option for Christians. Yet Mysticism, both ancient and modern, is *chock-full of SUPPOSED revelations from God!* In fact, this is its alluring drawing power. Its advocates promise: "*God will personally meet you* in the center of your soul and communicate directly to you matters *far beyond* anything found in Scripture." [165]

✓ **Example Number Five** brings us to Richard Foster, who is always careful to call mysticism "*Christian* meditation" or "*Christian* prayer"—even when *he knows full well* he's teaching exactly the SAME techniques and methods used by the ancient Hindu mystics and the modern New Age psychics, ALL of whom God condemns! Foster tells us, "*Christian meditation, very simply, is the ability to hear God's voice and obey His word.*" [166]

Here he is **NOT** advocating listening to the voice of God in the *written* revelation of inspired Scripture. He's not even equating the phrase *"His word"* with the Bible. He is speaking of hearing "God's voice"—supposedly—outside of the Scriptures, and obeying that revelation instead. He's not honoring or recommending God's written Word any more than his Quaker ancestor George Fox did. *For the "Silence" of Contemplative Prayer has **NO USE** for the Bible.*

Furthermore, in his books and conferences Richard Foster favorably quotes many leading mystics on the virtues and benefits of Contemplative Prayer, advancing the view that through it God "*offers you an understanding and light which are like nothing you **EVER** found in books or heard in sermons.*" [167]

Thus he promises "understanding and light" *far surpassing* anything found in Christian books, including **the Bible**, and *much, much better* than any message **EVER** heard in **church**. When he downplays and denigrates both the Bible and the church, it makes us wonder: Whose side is he on?

✓ **Example Number Six** awards ex-priest Brennan Manning a well-deserved place in this second category as he *mocks* a strong biblical position and whiningly complains to show his disdain for those who *do* have a high regard for God's Word:

> I am deeply distressed by what I can only call in our Christian culture *the idolatry of the Scriptures.* For many Christians, the Bible is not **a pointer TO** God but God **Himself**. In a word—*bibliolatry.* God cannot be confined within the covers of a leather-bound book. I develop a nasty rash around people who speak as if mere scrutiny of its pages will reveal precisely how God thinks and precisely what God wants. [168]

Baptist pastor David Cloud responds:

> Bible believers *don't worship* the Bible, but they *do* accept it for what it claims to be—the very Word of God—and they know therefore that they'll find on its pages **_precisely how God thinks!_** [169]

Manning also warns about "*academicians [professors* or *theologians]* who would imprison **Jesus** in the ivory tower of *exegesis* [that is, *explanation* or *analysis of a Bible text]*." [170]

Thus he sets up the authority of Jesus <u>against</u> that of the Bible, ignoring the fact that *we know nothing for certain about Jesus and His doctrine **apart from** the Bible!*

With his mind illuminated by mystical experiences, Brennan Manning describes God—the great God of heaven and earth—as being somewhat excessively sentimental or foolishly amorous. Some would even say "mushy":

> [Jesus] said, GOD IS LOVE — period. But there is MORE to the message of Jesus. He insisted that His Father is *crazy with love,* that *God is a kooky God* who can scarcely bear to be without us. [171]

And in his popular book, *The Signature of Jesus,* Manning devotes an entire chapter to Contemplative Prayer. He gives his readers the impression they're really missing out on God's love if they ignore this method of prayer. He calls this chapter **"Grabbing Aholt** [a hold] **of God."**

It is *blasphemous* to describe our holy God as "kooky." It is *deceptively misleading* to teach poor mortals they can "Grab Aholt" of the Most High God. But Brennan Manning is perfectly willing to stoop to using slangy, street-smart, degrading "lingo"—even putting such uncouth, unrefined terms into the mouth of *Jesus,* "the **King** of kings and **Lord** of lords" [172] —*IF* he thinks descending to "the lowest common denominator" will sell more books.

✓ **Example Number Seven** is Pastor Rick Warren, author of the best-sellers *The Purpose-Driven Church* and *The Purpose-Driven Life,* as well as being in charge of the Saddleback Church in Lake Forest, a city in Orange County, California—one of the megachurches of the world. He exerts a tremendous influence in Christian circles. And, unfortunately, he uses his influence on the side of Contemplative Prayer. He constantly promotes *contemplative authors* and their books and *mystical speakers* and their programs.

For instance, he glowingly praised Tricia Rhodes's book *The Soul at Rest: A Journey Into Contemplative Prayer* in his e-newsletter to thousands of pastors around the world, and then a few months later referred to Rhodes as "one of our favorite authors on Contemplative Prayer." [173]

But with this "favorite author" of Rick Warren, it's the same story as with all the other contemplatives. On the one hand, Tricia Rhodes *praises* Contemplative Prayer to the skies:

> Contemplative Prayer penetrates our heart of hearts, probing the deepest rooms of our interior soul. It leaves no stone unturned, no darkness unlit. . . . It is wonderful and painful and through it He changes us into His likeness. [174]

And on the other hand, Rhodes, like other fans of "the Silence," has very *limited* respect for the Bible:

> Reading, studying, or memorizing God's Word will take us only so far in our quest for spiritual growth. [175]

It seems that faith in Christ and dependence on the holy Scriptures is *just not enough—we need a trancelike mystical experience as well.*

Rick Warren personally has an extremely low regard for Bible prophecy, as revealed in this example of his teaching:

> When the disciples wanted to talk about prophecy, *Jesus quickly switched the conversation* to evangelism. He wanted them to concentrate on their mission in the world. He said in essence: *"The details of My return are none of your business.* What *IS* your business is the mission I've given you. Focus on that! . . . If you want [Me] to come back sooner, focus on fulfilling your mission, **NOT** *trying to figure out prophecy."* [176]

The words in quotes above are *NOT* a direct quotation from Jesus Christ—or from anyone else, anywhere. Instead, they are Warren's *completely imaginary interpretation* of the "essence" of our Lord's reply! Christian author Roger Oakland registers this "astounding" reaction to Rick Warren's presumptuous—and misleading—statement:

> I find it simply astounding that a statement of this sort would be in a *New York Times* best-seller in the present-day Christian book market. Jesus was telling His disciples they could not know the day or the hour, but **NOWHERE** does Jesus *EVER* indicate that *"the details of My return are none of your business."* Rather than quickly changing the subject, we find in **Matthew 24** and **Luke 21** two of the *LONGEST* passages in Scripture quoting Jesus' own words, as He **DETAILS** the signs of His Coming. . . . Later on, one of those disciples, John, was given an entire book to write [Revelation] on the details of Jesus coming. [177]

It's extremely hard to believe that **BOTH** the *author* **AND** the *editor(s)* at Zondervan—a publisher specializing in the Christian book market—were *totally ignorant* of Christ's pertinent words on prophecy in **Matthew 24:1–51** and **Luke 21:5–36**—a total of more than EIGHTY verses!

For Rick Warren, a prominent professional pastor, with years of training and experience, openly **DARES** not only to **deliberately MISQUOTE** but also to **directly CONTRADICT** the Lord Jesus Christ—God in the flesh, the Almighty Creator of heaven and earth—and **LIE to millions of readers in the process!** If he won't stop short of doing something like **THAT**, *what other evil* will he be bold enough to attempt?

✓ **Example Number Eight** is Eugene Peterson, another enthusiastic proponent of Contemplative Prayer, who was asked to work with Richard Foster as "Consulting Editor, New Testament" of the *Renovaré Spiritual Formation Bible* [178] after completing his own version of the Bible, *The Message*—which, by the way, is **NOT** *a verbal "translation" at all* but instead is as loose and liberal a *paraphrase* as one could imagine. Yet Rick Warren LIKES Peterson's kind of work in *The Message* so much that he quotes from it more than from any other version!

To feel Peterson's "spiritual pulse," simply note what he thinks about *the necessity of Bible study* for Christians:

> *Why do people spend so much time studying the Bible?* How much do you need to know? We invest all this time in understanding the text which has a separate life of its own, and we think we're being more pious and spiritual when we're doing it. . . . **[Christians] should be studying it LESS, not MORE.** You just need enough to pay attention to God. . . . *I'm just not at all pleased with all the emphasis on Bible study* as if it's some kind of special thing that Christians do, and the more they do the better. [179]

It *is* shocking, but *not* surprising, that Peterson esteems Bible study so little. While claiming to be a Greek and Hebrew scholar, Peterson regularly abandons definitions from *Strong's Concordance* and other trusted scholarly sources for his own poetic "translation" into today's "lingo."

God's Word, on the other hand, urges us to:

> **Study** to shew thyself approved unto God, a workman that needeth not to be ashamed, rightly dividing **the word of truth**. . . . ALL scripture is given by *inspiration of God,* and is profitable for *doctrine,* for *reproof,* for *correction,* for *instruction in righteousness:* That the man of God may be PERFECT, thoroughly furnished unto all good works. [180]

> ### D. Adopting False and Fatal Worldviews:
> ### Universalism • Monism • Pantheism • Panentheism

Richard Foster writes that the "testimony . . . by faithful believers throughout the centuries . . . is **amazingly uniform**" regarding mystic meditation![181]

That's the problem. The contemplative authors ARE "amazingly uniform." Listening to the spirit voices repeatedly whispering to them in "the Silence" of Contemplative Prayers has converted them **ALL** *uniformly* to a ***non-Christian*** ***worldview*** *of Universalism, Monism, Pantheism, and/or Panentheism!*

Let's pause for a moment to refresh our memories on these terms before we proceed any further.

Coming to Terms

universalism = The worldview or theological doctrine of <u>universal salvation</u>. Thus, a universalist believes that eternal salvation is extended to **ALL** <u>mankind</u> *regardless of one's belief or behavior.*

monism = The worldview based on the belief that *all* is ***ONE***, from the Greek *monos* ("one, single"). It asserts that ALL REALITY is *a unified whole*, that *everything* in the universe is composed of the same substance; ALL is organically ONE. No distinction at all exists between *Creator* and *creation.* Therefore, if *all is one,* then *all is God*—even man.

pantheism = The worldview based on the belief that all is God, from the Greek *pan* ("all") and *theos* ("God"). It asserts that *everything* in the universe *IS* God or is a *part* of God. Thus, a tree is God, a rock is God, and man is God. The conclusion is the same as in *monism,* but technically *pantheism* says, "All is *GOD*," while *monism* says, "All is *ONE*."

panentheism = The worldview based on the belief that "God is **IN** all things."

Let me explain:

One of the main New Age teachings is that God is *WITHIN* each person. And the New Age movement that seemed so radical in the sixties and seventies did not die out. We see it in the writings and hear it in the voices of those who proclaim the pagan worldviews of ***pantheism*** and ***panentheism***—two philosophies so close in meaning that they're *almost identical twins*—except for a slight difference. You see, *pantheism* is the belief that "ALL *IS* God" whereas *panentheism* is the belief that "God is *IN* all things."

Christian author Ray Yungen makes this observation:

The problem is that many well-intentioned people embrace the teachings of *panentheism* because it *sounds so good*. It appears *less bigoted* on God's part. *No one is left out*—all are connected to God. There is a great appeal in this message. Nevertheless, the Bible does *NOT* teach *universal* salvation for man. In contrast, Jesus said:

"You can enter God's Kingdom *ONLY* through the *narrow* gate. The highway to hell is *broad,* and its gate is *wide* for the *many* who choose the easy way. But the gateway to life is *small,* and the road is *narrow,* and only a *few* ever find it." [182]

Christ's message is *the polar opposite* of *universalist* teaching. God sent His Son, Jesus Christ, to die for the sins of the whole world. But *He did not say ALL would be saved,* because He knew some would reject the salvation He provided. "For the message of the cross is *foolishness* to those who are *perishing,* but to us who are being saved it is the power of God." [183]

Right here I should mention that all my life I've been a teacher. And as a teacher I try to explain things so clearly that they not only can be understood but that they **cannot** be **mis**understood. For instance, I would prefer to examine those four false worldviews *separately*—one at a time.

But I find that quite difficult when the mystical masters of Contemplative Prayer themselves *mix them all up* in their statements—sometimes mingling two or more worldviews together in a single sentence—as you may notice in several cases below.

With that warning, I hope you can follow safely through this minefield of error as I show you how **everyone** seduced into listening to spirit voices in "the Silence" *sooner or later migrates* from their true worldview of belief in God to "doctrines of demons," as Paul puts it in **1 Timothy 4:1.**

Henri Nouwen teaches *monism* when he writes:

Prayer is "soul work" because our souls are those sacred centers where **ALL is ONE**. . . . It is in the heart of God that we can come to the full realization of **the UNITY of ALL that is**. [184]

But then Nouwen, in the next quotation below, is compelled by his *panentheist* worldview to say "**IN**"—*twice!* But note that, at the end, he carefully and deliberately does *NOT* say "of each *Christian* believer." Instead, his *universalist* worldview is revealed by saying "**of each *human being*.**"

The God who dwells **IN *OUR*** inner sanctuary [as *Christian* believers in Jesus] is *ALSO the* **God who DWELLS IN *the inner sanctuary of EACH human being*.** [185]

John R. Yungblut, contemplative mystic and former dean of Studies at the Quaker Meditation Center at Pendle Hill in Pennsylvania, states the *monistic* "truth" felt by almost all contemplative practitioners:

The CORE of the mystical experience is the *feeling of UNITY,* and the *perception of RELATEDNESS*. For the **mystics** *the world is ONE*. [186]

Prolific Catholic writer Malachi Martin was himself a Jesuit priest until released to devote himself to writing, but he remained a priest all his life until his mysterious death in Manhattan in 1999. In his classic book, *The Jesuits,* Martin speaks of Loyola's passion for *mysticism* and, in the passage below, Loyola's very strong belief in *panentheism:*

> Each companion in the Society ("the Society of Jesus," also known simply as "the Jesuits") was burning and busy to find every trace of God and God's handiwork *throughout the cosmos. . . .* Of course, *I saw God at work* **IN ALL** *things*—vivifying, beautifying, freshening, and quickening human beings and all of nature into life-nourishing cycles. *Throughout, I thus saw* **God IN ALL** *things. . . . Nothing in creation could escape this viewpoint*—the fearful symmetry of the tiger, the ridiculous curl to a piglet's tail, perfumes, colors, tastes, the audible silence settled on mountaintops, the patterns traced by a dancer, the cries of children at play, the songs of birds, the toils of the least of insects. *Seeing ALL things in God,* with their being and their beauty, the scales would fall away from my flesh-bound eyes. *. . . Ignatius (Loyola) presumed that every Jesuit would have this same perpetual preoccupation with finding God in ALL things.* [187]

We can all admit that Malachi Martin is a very effective writer. And there is indeed beauty and great inspiration for all of us Christians in *recognizing* God as the divine, Almighty Creator! And *appreciating* His awesome handiwork in Nature can be *breathtaking* and *exhilarating*.

But let's be honest and candidly **REAL** here: There's a *world*—and a *worldview*—of *difference* between:

1. seeing God as *the* **Maker** *of all things, who exists* <u>above and beyond</u> *His magnificent Creation,* and having your love for Him thus enhanced by that humble and appreciative realization; and

2. believing deep down in your heart and mind that the Great God of heaven and earth is *actually, personally,* <u>located</u> **WITHIN** the petals of that tiny **flower** you hold in your hand—as well as **WITHIN** the **rock** out of whose crevice the flower grew!

So Ignatius Loyola and all other panentheists are dead *wrong*—wrong about where they place God's **LOCATION** in the universe. As the Almighty Creator, it logically follows that He existed **before** anything He created. By the same token, as it says in point 1 above, God as Creator "*exists* **<u>above and beyond</u>** *His magnificent Creation,*" **NOT INSIDE** *of it!* The pagan worldviews of the **EASTERN** religions may mislead some, but the Lord Jesus spoke the truth and settled the matter once and for all time when He prayed, "Our Father, **which art IN HEAVEN,**" [188] thereby confirming—as does the Bible as a whole—God's true location.

What we're dealing with here is a very important and vital issue. For one thing, churchgoers have a legitimate right to expect ministers posing as Christian spokesmen to teach a Christian worldview. That's simply a matter of basic ethics.

But here's why this issue of worldviews is so serious, so momentous: Remember that all sin originated with Lucifer when he rebelled against God in heaven, motivated by his prideful ambition to *"be like the Most High"* —Isaiah 14:14. And in **John 8:44** Jesus calls the devil *"the father of lies."* So we may safely assume that ALL false teachings—like these non-Christian worldviews—also have their origin with the devil, Satan.

Therefore, Christian author Ray Yungen shares this insight:

> It's important to understand that Satan is not simply trying to draw people to the dark side of a good-versus-evil conflict. Actually, *he's trying to eradicate the gap between himself and God, between good and evil, altogether.* . . . [Some spiritual leaders say God is IN] **ALL** things. *All means all*—nothing left out. Such reasoning implies that God has given His glory to **ALL** of creation; since Satan is *part of* creation, then he, too, shares in this glory, and thus is *"like the Most High."* [189]

So those voices of evil spirits that indoctrinate unsuspecting people in "the Silence" with these *false worldviews* serve Satan's strategy quite well. *But not only that.* You'll recall that **Satan's plan has *always* been to deceive people into thinking *THEY* can become God,** and God has given Satan the freedom to carry out his diabolical plans so that they may be seen for what they really are. In the Garden of Eden, the Serpent spoke to only one person, Eve, when he lied and told her that in the day she eats of the forbidden fruit, "your eyes will be opened, and ***you will be like God,*** knowing good and evil." [190] But today Satan has **thousands** opening themselves up to Contemplative Prayer and believing his mystical, devilish lies—just as Shirley MacLaine really but mistakenly believes that *she IS God!*

Of course, if panentheism were true, if God Himself were **really** WITHIN each and every single one of us—as many, many people quoted on these pages teach in all seriousness—then salvation through a Redeemer would become unnecessary and Jesus' death on the Cross would be rendered altogether futile and pointless. Still, that apparently doesn't matter in some circles. Read on.

Trappist monk and mystic Basil Pennington not only believes in the panentheistic "**God within**" concept himself but presents that idea to us in his book, *Awake in the Spirit,* where he speaks of *our "process of deification."* [191]

New Age leader and Episcopal priest Matthew Fox is one fellow not bashful at all about touting his mystical panentheistic views. He expresses them quite strongly and openly in his book, *The Coming of the Cosmic Christ:* "*Divinity* is found **IN ALL** creatures. . . . The Cosmic Christ is the '**I AM**' **IN EVERY** creature." [192] Furthermore, Fox tells us that Jesus is someone "who shows us **how to embrace** *our own DIVINITY.*" [193]

On the back cover of his book Fox blasphemously advocates that there should be a "**shift AWAY FROM the historical Jesus**" and *more attention* given to the "**cosmic Christ**" who is **WITHIN** each one of us!

Catholic monk and teacher of Eastern mysticism Thomas Merton made clear his *panentheist* ("God is **IN** all things") view when he said: "True solitude is a participation in the solitariness of **God—Who is IN ALL things.**" [194]

On the other hand, Merton apparently was also a *pantheist* who believed that "God **IS** all." Please note:

> The contemplative experience is neither a UNION of separate identities nor a FUSION of them; on the contrary, *separate identities disappear* in the **ALL Who is God.** [195]

Conspicuous by its ABSENCE in all these startling pronouncements is the glaring **LACK** of any Scripture texts from the Bible to prove the claims made by these "religious teachers" and "spiritual leaders." We needn't wonder whether or not they *have* any Bible backing, for if they ever *found* any, you can be sure they'd broadcast it loudly!

Brennan Manning, in his book *Abba's Child,* recommends the writings of Beatrice Bruteau, calling her a "trustworthy guide to contemplative consciousness." Who is Beatrice Bruteau and what does she believe? She is the founder of **THE SCHOOL FOR CONTEMPLATION,** and she believes that God is **WITHIN** every human being. She wrote the book, *What We Can Learn from the EAST,* and says that *each person* can claim to be "I AM"—which is a special name for Almighty God—explaining:

> *We have realized OURSELVES as the Self that says only I AM, with no predicate following,* not "I am a this" or "I have that quality." Only unlimited, absolute "**I AM.**" [196]

Of course, "I AM" is one of the Lord's most sacred biblical names, as He is the *everlasting, ever-present God.* [197] And Bruteau is *very much aware* of that fact, which is precisely *why* she urges all of us to say that. But why would Manning recommend Bruteau *with no warning* if he does not agree with this blasphemy? When he says she is "trustworthy," does he mean we can trust her when she says *we are all* I AM?

One tragic, but typical, true story may be enough to show how Contemplative Prayer can *completely change one's worldview 180 degrees!*—from that of a Sunday school teacher to that of a New Age goddess worshiper who *hates* the Bible. Please note:

Years ago, popular author Sue Monk Kidd was an active member in her Baptist church. Then, suffering a deep hollowness and spiritual hunger, she underwent a transformation of belief when, ironically enough, *a Sunday school co-worker handed her a book by Thomas Merton and told her she needed to read it.* Her life changed dramatically as she read *numerous* Contemplative Prayer books and repeated her "sacred word" *mantras* as her reading taught.[198]

In time, she came to the mystical conclusion of *monism* (All is ONE) and *panentheism* (God is IN All) that:

> "I am speaking of recognizing the *hidden* [*occult*] truth that <u>we are **ONE** with **ALL** people</u>. We are *part of them* and they are *part of us.* . . . When we encounter another person, . . . we should walk as if we were upon holy ground. We should respond as if **God dwells there.**"[199]

Now—in defense of Sue Monk Kidd—I must say that *of course* we need to treat all people well and recognize that we all share a common humanity. As children of God, our heavenly Father, we are all brothers and sisters— and we should love each other as such. But those four false worldviews listed above are *seriously mistaken* when they fail to distinguish between Christians and non-Christians, believers and unbelievers—thereby <u>negating</u> Christ's imperative: "<u>Ye must be born again</u>" (**John 3:7**), as the prerequisite for the indwelling of God.

Monk Kidd's *panentheism* is easily apparent when she approvingly quotes someone who advises that the *Hindu* greeting *namaste,* offered with a reverential bow, and which translates, *"I honor the god in you,"* should be used by *Christians.*[200]

Monk Kidd wrote her first and second books from a Christian perspective, but with her third and fourth books, she made a sharp turn to a spiritual view more in tune with the witchcraft of Wicca than with Christianity. Now, as a *pantheist,* she worships the goddess Sophia and Nature rather than the Lord Jesus Christ:

> "We need *Goddess consciousness* to reveal **earth's holiness**. . . . **Matter** becomes *inspirited; it breathes* **divinity. Earth** becomes *alive* and **sacred**. . . . *Goddess* offers us the **HOLINESS** of everything."[201]

Christian writer and apologist Ray Yungen, in his excellent exposé of the dangers posed to Christianity by Contemplative Prayer, shares in his book *A Time of Departing* another bit of Sue Monk Kidd's thinking, as he says, "No one can lightly dismiss or ignore the powers behind Contemplative Prayer after reading this narrative" that Kidd wrote in her book *The Dance of the Dissident Daughter: A Woman's Journey From Christian Tradition to the Sacred Feminine.* [202] Here is her brief story:

> The minister was preaching. He was holding up a Bible. . . . He was saying that the Bible was the sole and ultimate authority of the Christian's life. The *sole* and *ultimate* authority.
>
> I remember a **FEELING** rising up. . . . It was a passionate, determined feeling, and it spread out from the core of me like a current so that my skin *vibrated* with it. If feelings could be translated into English, this feeling would have roughly been the word *no!*
>
> It was the purest inner knowing I had experienced, and it was shouting in me *no, no, no!* The ultimate authority in **MY** life is **NOT the Bible;** it is not confined between the covers of a book. It is not something written by men and frozen in time. *It is NOT from a source OUTSIDE MYSELF. My ultimate authority is the **DIVINE** voice **IN MY OWN soul.*** Period. [203]

Scripture Text #4: Luke 17:21 *

* To those readers who note that the discussion of this fourth text is *separated* from the other three refuted above, let me say that I purposely reserved it to this point simply because *it affords the **correction** of a widespread misconception* which is needed right here.

In **Luke 17:21,** KJV, Jesus said, *"The kingdom of God is within you."* Those who hold the worldview of *panentheism* (or even *pantheism* or *monism*) seize on the word *within* to support their belief. Most other Bible scholars and theologians are not at all willing to accept their interpretation—for good reason.

You see, the original Greek word Jesus used was *entos,* which may mean *"within"* OR *"among"* OR *"in the midst of"* in English. And in fact different Bible versions have translated this verse all three ways—the King James Version says *within,* and most other versions say the other two ways. So *which* translation is *correct?* Did Jesus tell those He was addressing that the kingdom was **within** them, **among** them, or **in the midst of** them?

A Good Rule: "Consider the Context"

Someone once wisely said: "A **text** *taken out of* **context** is a **pretext**." You see, words don't exist in a vacuum. There are always certain factors or surrounding elements involved, such as **what** was said, **to whom** it was said, **when** and **why** it was said, and so forth. In our endeavor to determine the true meaning of a Bible text, we need to *look at the whole picture*—which is called its CONTEXT.

So far, we know only one element: we know **WHAT** was said in Greek. But its translation into English offers *three perfectly valid choices*. Fortunately, there **IS** a way to determine which of those translations Jesus meant, **without a doubt!** We need only determine *the persons being addressed* to find which translation is the best choice suited to *them*.

In **Luke 17:21** Jesus was addressing the unsaved Pharisees, the Lord's greatest opponents. They not only **did not believe in Him** but actively plotted to **kill Him**, *so how could the kingdom of God be within them?*

Jesus was certainly **NOT** saying that the kingdom of God was inside of them, for on another occasion[204] He told the Pharisees that their father was the devil. And note Christ's words here:

> "**Woe to you**, teachers of the law and **Pharisees, you hypocrites!** *You shut the door of the kingdom of heaven in people's faces. You yourselves do not enter, nor will you let those enter who are trying to.*"[205]

Thus the Pharisees had **NO** relation to the kingdom of God. And therefore we can confidently state that this translation—"the kingdom of God is **WITHIN** you"—is a bad choice. It misleads readers throughout Christendom where many believe that the kingdom is **within** the hearts of those Pharisees—and themselves.

The *better* translation, the *more accurate* translation, is: "The kingdom of God is **in your midst**" or "is **among** you." For, again, if we *consider the context* and look at the whole scene, we see Jesus (the King) with His disciples (the kingdom) talking to unbelievers who perhaps were all mingled together and in the midst of each other. The Master was saying, to those hard-hearted Pharisees: "Open your eyes and see—the kingdom of God is *right here in your midst, here among you, if you could only see it!*"

Yet some may object and say, "But wait a minute! Christ *could* have been addressing His disciples—who **WERE** faithful believers, and who therefore could be said to have the kingdom **WITHIN** them!"

No, that's not a valid option—because the Bible won't allow it. You see, **Luke 17:21**, which is the text at issue, lies between verse **20** and **22**. And verse **20** says *Christ was asked a question "by the Pharisees."* It also says, "He answered **THEM**" in speaking about the kingdom of God. So we know He was not addressing His disciples.

Furthermore, verse **22** begins by saying plainly and *in distinction to* the verse before: "**THEN** [*or, depending on the Bible version* "**AND**"] He said **to His DISCIPLES** . . ." Since the Scripture gives no details here, that subsequent message to His disciples could well have followed at a *later time* and at a *different place*.

Though some interpreters are *tempted* to use this verse for their own selfish purposes rather than for elucidating the Bible—and they're *willing* to rip it from its context to achieve that purpose—the evidence seems strongly against translating it "**within**."

"Location, Location, Location!"

The heading immediately above is the emphatic expression of a business rule that cannot be stated too strongly. Young businessmen eager to learn "the tricks of the trade" are taught always to make the vital element of *location* a key part of their planning.

Thus someone planning to build a huge manufacturing plant building motor cars or jet aircraft is wise to consider its location relative to the *raw materials needed* and also its convenient proximity to a large *labor force to work there*.

By the same token, someone planning to open a new department store or restaurant or other commercial endeavor should take location into account and study in advance whether the nearby population is large enough to supply potential customers and also whether competing vendors have already preempted the territory. It would be a mistake to build a huge hospital and medical center in the middle of the desert where no one lives.

So location is obviously of vital importance in *business,* just as Truth is vital in *religion*. And the teachers of mystic meditation, by following "the father of lies" and teaching **panentheism**, have fallen short on **BOTH** counts:

They have NOT told us the Truth about the Location of God!

But praise the Lord that Jesus—the Master Teacher—taught us to pray to God **in Heaven**, *NOT* to God **INSIDE of US!** He said: *"After this manner therefore PRAY YE:* 'Our Father which art IN HEAVEN, Hallowed be Thy name.' " —**Matthew 6:9.**

Right there—in the very opening words of His model Prayer—Jesus put us on the right track. Evidently, Christ understood how important **LOCATION** is and wanted that to be part of His teaching to us. He didn't want us to "dial a wrong number" and get connected to the *wrong party!*

The Lord Jesus, who surely knew better than anyone else, unhesitatingly and repeatedly spoke of a realm, a kingdom called "heaven" as if *it is indeed a real, tangible, matter-of-fact **place*** where He and His **heavenly** Father jointly reign—and where their throne is *LOCATED!*

Among many examples, even in that same perfect Prayer given as a model, Christ urged us to pray to the Father that His will be done *"On earth **as it is in Heaven**."* —**Matthew 6:10.** And again, in **Matthew 6:19–20,** Jesus tells us:

"Do **NOT** lay up for yourselves **treasures on EARTH,** where moth and rust destroy and where thieves break in and steal; but lay up for yourselves **treasures in HEAVEN,** where neither moth nor rust destroys and where thieves do not break in and steal. For where your treasure is, there your heart will be also."

In this world of *religious pluralism,* pagan religions still exist with their false theologies. As Paul teaches so clearly in **1 Corinthians 8:5–6,** "Even if there are **so-called gods,** whether in heaven or on earth (as there are **MANY GODS** and **MANY LORDS**), yet for us there is one God, the Father, . . . and one Lord Jesus Christ."

But false theologies teach faulty worldviews that lead us astray. Some of those worldviews use terms which may be new to us, so let me make a clear distinction between the words **transcendent** and **immanent.**

Immanent means existing **within** or inherent **within.** Hinduism believes and teaches that its god Brahman is *immanent* in human beings—*AND in everything else!* (Hence the faulty worldviews of *monism, pantheism,* and *panentheism*).

Transcendent, however, means **above** and **beyond** the material universe. Orthodox Christianity is worlds—or worldviews—apart from Hinduism in believing not in the *immanence* of God but in His *transcendence.* Bible-believing Christians understand and teach that there's a great distinction between the Creator and His very real creation—that God is *above* and *beyond* the things He has made, "though He is *not far* from each one of us." [206]

Thus Christians worship the great Creator God who reigns transcendent above all things. Yet there is, paradoxically enough, one sense in which they find Him at times to be *both* immanent *and* transcendent! You see, because of their understanding of the Holy Trinity, they know that the divine presence of the Holy Spirit can indwell believers.

But even though the inspired Word of God offers no support for the false worldview of *panentheism,* that doesn't stop its promoters. For, regardless of what God says in His Word, it seems that *panentheism*—the fiction that the great God of the Universe *resides WITHIN us* and that, therefore, **WE** are **God**—is the very **BEDROCK** of the New Age and Contemplative Prayer movements.

Let's see some examples of this revolutionary, blasphemous idea.

Sue Monk Kidd, mentioned above, began her spiritual life as a Sunday School teacher and then became seduced into the mysticism of Contemplative Prayer. Did this seemingly harmless "experience" alter her worldview in any radical way? Listen to her now, and realize that *she is deadly serious,* for *she honestly, truly believes* what she's saying:

> I came to **KNOW** myself as an **embodiment** of **Goddess**. . . . *Transcendence* and *immanence* are **NOT** separate. The Divine is **ONE**. . . . The day of my awakening was the day I *saw* and **KNEW** I *saw all things in God,* and **God IN all things**. [207]

Richard Foster, in his original 1978 edition of *Celebration of Discipline,* wrote, "Christian meditation is an attempt to empty the mind in order to fill it." [208] *Fill it with what?* In *EASTERN* religions a person empties his mind in order to become ONE with the universe (or the "Cosmic Mind"). In so-called Christian mysticism one empties the mind in order to become ONE with God—**who is found, by the way, *IN OURSELVES!*** [209]

Richard Foster quotes, with approval, many other "far out" mystics. For example, there is Russian mystic Theophan the Recluse, who said,

> To pray is to ***DESCEND with the mind INTO the heart***, and there to stand before the face of **the Lord, ever-present**, all-seeing, ***WITHIN you.*** [210]

Another is Madame Guyon (1648–1717) who was a French Catholic mystic and one of the key advocates of *Quietism.* Quietism was considered heretical by the Roman Catholic Church, and she was imprisoned from 1695 to 1703 after publishing a book on the topic, *A Short and Easy Method of Prayer.* Her life was devoted to the mysticism and "Silence" of Contemplative Prayer—with the resulting worldviews of *pantheism* and *panentheism.* She makes this confession of her faith: "Here [in the contemplative state] **everything *IS* God. God is everywhere and IN all things**." [211]

Since this study on Contemplative Prayer deals with a religious subject, and most religious doctrines originate with professional clergy, most of those mentioned have been Catholic monks who had plenty of time to experiment with mystical practices, as well as Protestant ministers and writers who also served as grassroots in their domain.

But I want you to understand that the New Age and Contemplative Prayer movements *affect the rank and file of ALL people*; even those far away from the cloistered life of monasteries and churches. For instance, Shirley MacLaine, Oprah Winfrey, and Sue Monk Kidd enjoy celebrity status in the movies, television, and as professional writers—but they're not working directly in organized religion. The point is that these religious ideas reach "ordinary" people in every walk of life—people who take these religious ideas very, very seriously.

One example of such people is Dr. Dean Ornish, a California medical doctor and internist who wrote the best-selling book on healthful living,

Dr. Dean Ornish's Program for Reversing Heart Disease. Interesting from our point of view is the fact that Dr. Ornish is known for promoting the **Hindu practice of yoga** as part of his program to treat patients with cardiac problems. The spiritual precepts behind yoga are blatantly occultic, but Dr. Ornish believes so much in the worldviews of *panentheism* and *pantheism* (as do most yoga advocates) that he claims: *"Everyone and everything IS God in disguise."* [212]

Another example is M. Scott Peck, MD (1936–2005), who was a psychiatrist and, in 1978, author of one of the bestselling books of all time, *The Road Less Traveled*. LIFE magazine called it a "national institution" and compared its selling power to that of the Bible.

The Road Less Traveled takes its title from a poem of the same name by Robert Frost. It's a book even Christians could approve—until they reached Peck's question "What does God **want** from us?" and then his answer, "It is for the individual to **become totally, wholly, <u>God</u>**." [213] Readers troubled by such a statement could not yet know of Peck's journey into the New Age—not until they read his later statements such as these: "Zen Buddhism should be taught in every 5th grade class in America." [214]

In an interview with *New Age* magazine, Peck said that there are "an enormous number of people who have a passion for God, but they are *fed up to the gills with fundamentalism.*" The interview also divulged that Peck moved from "*EASTERN* mystical religions [especially Buddhism] toward [so-called!] *Christian mysticism* [Contemplative Prayer]." [215]

In his book *A World Waiting to Be Born*, Peck noted the necessity of Contemplative Prayer:

> *This process of EMPTYING the MIND is of such importance* it will continue to be a significant theme. . . . It may help to remember, therefore, that the purpose of emptying the mind is not ultimately to have *nothing* there; rather it is to make room in the mind for something new, something unexpected, to come in. What *IS* the something new? *It is the voice of God*. [216]

He also writes that Jesus was merely "an example of the Western *MYSTIC* [who] integrated himself with God," that Jesus' message to us was "cease clinging to our *lesser selves* [and find] our greater *true selves*." Contemplative Prayer "is a lifestyle dedicated to maximum awareness." [217]

In 1995, two writers who tried to give a fair, neutral report on M. Scott Peck's teaching could ultimately arrive only at this conclusion:

> Peck is echoing a concept found in Hinduism and Buddhism, namely, that **ALL reality is ONENESS** [*monism*] and that what we perceive as individuality is an *illusion* [*maya*]. . . . The above concept is a

major tenet of the New Age movement. . . . Like all New Agers, Peck embraces the belief that realization of **our oneness with God**—or our own godhood—is essential to spiritual growth and freedom from problems. Attaining **GODHOOD** is the only reason we exist. Realization of **our DIVINITY** is also *the whole purpose behind evolution,* which is another **"miracle"** to Peck. [218]

Dr. M. Scott Peck, certainly by any worldly standard, must be considered "a guy who's got it made!" After all, he was a respected member of his chosen profession, a multimillionaire from his books, and a gentleman who was looked upon with favor by many. Yet before he turned to Christ and began even a cursory reading of God's Word, he had already immersed himself for years in the beliefs and practices of Zen Buddhism.

Consequently, he was impregnated with a philosophy and worldview which he was *never able to shake off,* for his inner **MIND** had become **infected** through the dark mystic avenue of Contemplative Prayer and the "seducing spirits" he had listened to in "the Silence."

Yet none of that matters to some people. That's why journalist Michael D'Antonio, in his book *Heaven on Earth,* wrote that he saw Peck as "the Billy Graham of the New Age . . . a major New Age leader." [219]

As we leave M. Scott Peck, please take this word of caution that much of his advice in his "self-help" books is tainted with the mystical and occult.

I'll give one more example of exactly what I mean: Take, for instance, Robert Schuller, retired pastor of the Crystal Cathedral in Garden Grove, California. Gray hair like a friendly grandfather. Nice smile. Kindly demeanor. Masterful use of words makes anyone think *he really knows* what he's talking about. So we confidently *TRUST* him. *Now look at what he taught* as early as 1977—but as you do, as one whose eyes have been opened, try to keep in mind *ALL that you've learned in these pages:*

> A variety of approaches to meditation . . . is employed by *many different religions* as well as by various non-religious mind-control systems. **In ALL forms** . . . TM, Zen Buddhism, or Yoga or . . . meditation . . . of Judaeo-Christian tradition . . . *the meditator endeavors to overcome the distractions of the conscious mind.* . . .

> It is important to remember that meditation in **ANY** form is the harnessing, by human means, of God's divine laws. . . . We are endowed with a great many **powers and forces that we do not yet fully understand.**

> The **most effective** mantras employ the "M" sound. You can get the feel of it by repeating the words "I am, I am, I am," many times over. . . . Transcendental Meditation is *NOT* a religion NOR is it necessarily anti-Christian. [220]

Contradicting Schuller's last sentence, both Christian authors of *The Seduction of Christianity* say: "TM is in fact **pure Hinduism**, and will lead to eternal separation from Christ." [221] And we already saw how the U.S. Court of Appeals upheld a lower court's decision in declaring Transcendental Meditation "**Hindu religion**"—also in direct contradiction to Schuller. And the demons must chuckle at Schuller's teaching innocent, trusting souls to use God's sacred name. How *blasphemous* of Schuller, for *he surely must know better*.

In the *Be Still* DVD, Richard Foster says that *ANYONE* can practice Contemplative Prayer and become a "portable sanctuary" for God. [222] This backs up other statements by Foster over the course of the past thirty years in which he believes that *even a non-believer in Christ* can participate in the "spiritual discipline" of silence and have an encounter with God. *The assumption by all mystics is that God dwells in ALL people, and meditation will help them to realize their own Divinity.* This panentheistic view of God is very typical for contemplatives. Those who practice contemplative prayer begin to view God through *panentheistic* (God is **IN** all) and *interspiritual* (all is united) eyes.

Thomas Merton, whom Foster has admired publicly for many years, believed that ALL human beings have divinity within, and this divinity can be *accessed* through Contemplative Prayer, thereby making the cross of Jesus unnecessary for union with God. We believe that the reason for this CHANGE in spiritual outlook for those who continue practicing contemplative meditation (*i.e.,* mantra meditation) is that *these altered states of consciousness actually ENGAGE the practitioner with DEMONIC realms leading to spiritual deception.*

A DIVINE PREDICTION COME TRUE!

Many times we don't fully grasp the essence of a divine prediction until we actually SEE its fulfillment. An example of this is found in **Matthew 24:5**, where Christ answers His disciples' question from **verse 3** about what signs will point to His second coming and the end of the world. Jesus said: "Many will come in My name, saying, 'I am the Christ,' and will deceive many."

Christian author Ray Yungen—whose first book, not coincidentally, was entitled *Many Shall Come in My Name*—points out that the Greek word for "many" in Christ's answer is *polus,* which means a *very great* number. It may actually mean that millions upon millions of people are going to claim deity for themselves!

Yungen explains further that the *remainder* of that prophetic verse tells us that *they will actually say:* "**I am Christ**"! [223]

Now I had read that verse many times, and I believed it. But I had always thought it referred to a few misled folks like Shirley MacLaine, Jim Jones of the Jonestown suicides, and David Koresh of the Waco tragedy. They all boldly and blasphemously claimed to be God or Christ—but they're only a few. Still, even though Jesus said "many" *(polus)*, I thought those few must suffice as a fulfillment of His prophecy.

But *now*—with *thousands* upon misled thousands *consenting* to go into "the Silence," consenting to **empty** the only mind God ever gave them, *consenting* to listen to spirit voices whispering false worldviews that deceive—Satan is gaining **countless** converts to his New Age theology! Here are some examples of what they say, believe, and teach so emphatically:

> The Christ is You. You are the one who is to come—**each of you. Each and everyone of you!** [224]

> Christhood is **NOT** something to come at a point in the future when you are more evolved. **Christhood is—right now! I am the Christ of God. You are the Christ of God.** [225]

Yet those victims of Contemplative Prayer who end up with insane worldviews, saying *"I am God"* or *"I am Christ"* don't have a biblical leg to stand on. For it was the serpent in Eden who lyingly promised, "You shall be like God" (**Genesis 3:5**)—on condition of Adam and Eve's *disobeying*. On the other hand, God **NEVER** promised man **DEITY**. Eternal life, yes (**Romans 6:23**). But—even when given immortality in heaven, where no one ever dies—we do not become **DIVINE!** Those listening to panentheistic voices in the Silence are dangerously deceived.

The German Willigis Jager is both a Benedictine monk and a master of Zen Buddhism, but despite being a long-standing member of the professional clergy, he makes this mistaken assertion about **Luke 17:21** in his book *Contemplation: A Christian Path,*

> Salvation will now be *NOTHING* other than a realization of the fact that *"the kingdom of God is within you."* . . . This is the Good News Jesus proclaimed to humanity. **The kingdom is already WITHIN ALL of us.** [226]

More than that, you can see that as a spiritual teacher Jager is a strong advocate for both *panentheism* and *universalism,* either of which could lead one fatally astray. Finally, he could be accused of false advertising in the title of his book, for the "contemplation" he teaches is *anything but* "Christian."

God Warns Us Against "Seducing Spirits"

The apostle Paul by divine Inspiration warns that in the last days before Jesus' second coming *"some shall depart from the faith, giving heed to SEDUCING SPIRITS, and DOCTRINES of DEVILS."* [227]

In this connection—and in strong refutation of the false worldview of *monism*—author Ray Yungen wrote that:

> *IF* what Henri Nouwen proclaimed is true when he said, "We can come to *the full realization* of **the UNITY of ALL** that is," [228] *THEN* Jesus Christ and Satan are also united. *That* is something only a demonic spirit would teach! [229]

Yungen adds that an even more subtle yet seductive idea says: Without a mystical technique (*like Contemplative Prayer!*), God is somehow **indifferent** or **unapproachable**. But if we're parents, we can plainly see the falsehood of this. *Do your children need to employ a method or engage in a ritual to capture your full attention?* Of course not! If you love your children, you'll care for them because you're committed to them and want to help them. The same is true of God's attention toward those He calls His own.

But once a spiritual seeker steps onto the slippery slope of Contemplative Prayer and its sure result of dangerous worldviews, he or she *keeps going down, unable stop*—or even *not wanting* to stop—until in the end faith in Jesus Himself is lost and all hope of heaven is also lost!

Note, for example, how the Catholic priest and mystic teacher Henri Nouwen ended up. By worldly standards he seemed to have a successful life—as a popular author and respected professor. But something had vanished inside—whatever Christian faith he once may have had was gone.

In his final book, Henri Nouwen confessed his faith—*NOT* so much faith in *Jesus* but in his adopted philosophy of *universalism / pantheism:*

> Today I personally believe that while Jesus came to open the door to God's house, **ALL** *human beings* can walk through that door, *whether they KNOW about Jesus or NOT*. Today I see it as my call to help *EVERY* person claim *his or her* **OWN** *way to God*. [230]

John R. Yungblut, contemplative author and former dean of Studies at the **QUAKER MEDITATION CENTER** at Pendle Hill in Pennsylvania, echoes a similar notion. Since mystic practitioners end up believing that ALL people are divine and ALL are entitled to say, "I am Christ," then:

> We CANNOT *CONFINE* the existence of the **DIVINE** to this one man [Jesus] among men. Therefore we are *NOT* to **worship** the man Jesus, *though we cannot refrain from worshiping the* **source** of this Holy Spirit or Christ-life which for many of us has been revealed primarily in this historical figure. [231]

Near the end of his life, it was perfectly clear that Thomas Merton had a severe case of *panentheism*. And he had it . . . *BAD!* In witness of that, he left this testimony:

It is a glorious destiny to be a member of the human race. . . . Now I realize **what we ALL ARE**. . . . If only they [people] could **ALL** see themselves **as they really ARE**, . . . I suppose the big problem would be that **we would fall down and WORSHIP each other**. . . . At the center of *our being* is a point of *nothingness* which is *untouched by sin* and by illusions, a point of pure truth. . . . This little point . . . is the pure glory of **God IN us**. **It is IN everybody**. [232]

Reading some of the statements made by those in the mystical meditative movement may make us think: "These people are *CRAZY!*" But they're not. Most of them are quite accomplished and intelligent. Yet their *minds* have been affected in the same way hallucinogenic drugs affect them. Their minds have been affected—and *infected*—by those unworldly *worldviews* that are *NOT based on the gospel truth of the Bible*. Their consciousness—excuse me, their *altered* consciousness—has been *invaded by spirits from another realm* who have planted thoughts and dreams and lies they would never have entertained for a moment—at the *beginning* of their downward path.

Philip St. Romain, a substance-abuse counselor and devout Catholic lay minister, wrote a book about his journey into Contemplative Prayer called *Kundalini Energy and Christian Spirituality*. He experienced "the lights! The gold swirls . . . began to intensify." He felt "prickly sensations" on the top of his head, and at times it—his head—would "fizzle with energy"—a sensation that would *go on for days!*

Most people believe St. Romain is a devout Christian. He still attends church. What has *changed*, though, are his sensibilities. He says:

I **CANNOT** make *any decisions* for myself **WITHOUT** the approbation [approval] of the **inner adviser**, whose voice speaks so clearly. . . . there is a distinct sense of **an inner eye** of some kind "seeing" with my two sense eyes. [233]

It seems clear that St. Romain's **MIND** has been "taken over" by "another power." An otherwise intelligent adult can't make his own decisions but is **POSSESSED** by another spirit. *How needlessly tragic!*

We need to reflect upon what God says in **Hebrews 13:9**, NIV—"Do *NOT* be **carried away** by all kinds of **strange teachings.**"

You see, **IF** God had **wanted** us to encounter Him through mystical practices such as Contemplative Prayer, **THEN why did He not SAY so?** Why did He not give **examples** and **instructions?** How could the Holy Spirit inspire the writing of the Scriptures yet *forget* to include a chapter or two on mysticism, spiritual exercises, and meditation of the **Eastern** variety?

Are we to believe that all of this is a great oversight, a huge "oops" on God's part to have left out such vital instructions on an *indispensable* experience that is *absolutely essential* to Christian spirituality? Then, having realized what He had done, are we to believe that God—*centuries later*—revealed this *missing ingredient* of Christian living to Roman Catholic monks, where it was *rejected* by the Reformers, only to have Richard Foster *re-introduce* it to the twentieth century? All this is quite hard to swallow—but apparently it's being accepted by many today. [234]

To sum it all up, let's simply ask: Is Contemplative Prayer *biblical?* Is it *Christian?* Anyone who takes a good, hard look at the evidence knows the answer: It is certainly **NOT** either one of those.

For it's much too *mystical* to be **biblical**. And it's much more *Hindu* and *Buddhist*—and *New Age*—than **Christian**.

If Satan has any WMDs ("Weapons of Mass Destruction"), then Contemplative Prayer is certainly one of them! For any way you look at it, it's **devilishly dangerous** to both the **church** collectively and the **Christian** individually.

The Lord God Himself declares in **Jeremiah 5:30–31**,

> "An astonishing and **horrible** thing has been committed in the land: *The PROPHETS prophesy **falsely**, and the PRIESTS rule by their **own** power;* and **My people *LOVE* to have it so**. *But what will you do **in the end?***"

TRUTH AND FALSEHOOD: POLAR OPPOSITES

There's a great difference, a vast contrast, between Truth and falsehood. Our Almighty God is the Author of Truth. [235] But the devil is the father of lies. [236] For those who accept and believe, God's Truth can be life-giving— but lies can be deadly.

Truth is mighty. But it is not only extremely powerful; it is also enduring and everlasting. God's truth—like *mathematical* truth—is *unchanging:* **2 + 2** is *always* **4,** and **3 X 3** is *always* **9.** Yet even in a world of constant change, the Bible says,

"The *grass withers,* the *flower fades,*
But *the Word of our God stands forever."* [237]

In stark contrast, every falsehood, every lie, is merely *an illusion of an illusion.* It has *no reality in fact at all* but instead is nothing but a twisted figment of imagination in the mind of some poor, misled mortal. [238] A genuine lie (I won't say "true" lie!), has *absolutely no substance* in the world as we know it.

For if we analyze a lie carefully, if we scrutinize the details of its *baseless claims,* we soon realize its *insubstantial nature,* and see that there is indeed *"nothing to it!"*

My prayer, therefore, is that readers will **SEE** Spiritual Formation, Contemplative Prayer, and the Emerging Church *for what they really are*—diabolical lies without a smidgen of Truth to them. They are, in fact, among the *DEADLIEST* falsehoods ever conceived in the evil mind of "the father of lies." And that, my friends, is what makes them so terribly dangerous and deceptive!

In closing, our loving God tells us exactly what to do in just a few words—quoted here from the pen of Paul:

"Have *NO* **FELLOWSHIP**
with the unfruitful works of **DARKNESS,**
but rather *EXPOSE* them." [239]

Perhaps the modern church has neglected the spiritual side of the Christian faith in favor of good ol' American business savvy to "grow" our churches. As a result, many church leaders may seldom give much thought to the very real *spiritual* side of the Christian faith.

And Satan has slithered into this void to exploit undiscerning believers. *The mind-altering spiritual poison* of Eastern-grown Transcendental Meditation—also known as Contemplative Prayer—has begun to seep deeply into the very mainstream of our Lord's Church. Believers everywhere should feel grave concern over this *Emerging Mysticism!*

Taken together, the Emerging Church and Contemplative Prayer promise Christianity nothing but *double trouble.*

+ + +

Now, having examined the facts, we can conclude only that Spiritual Formation—with its mystical "Silence" of Contemplative Prayer in the Emerging Church—is <u>a modern-day **"Trojan Horse"**</u> quietly smuggled into Christianity by the devil himself. *And we don't want **any part** of it!*

The bottom line on Contemplative Prayer is . . .

- It can't be proved from the Bible.
- It's not from God but from Satan.

～

Notes

1. An example of the degree to which each Jesuit must submit his mind and will to his superiors is seen in Loyola's *Spiritual Exercises* under the heading: "TO HAVE THE TRUE SENTIMENT WHICH WE OUGHT TO HAVE IN THE CHURCH MILITANT" and its "THIRTEENTH RULE. *To be right in everything, we ought always to hold that the WHITE which I see, is BLACK, if the Hierarchical [Roman Catholic] Church so decides it.*" There are eighteen such rules under this one small heading alone, and several other headings or sections in Loyola's book. —From the Official Web site: http://www.sacred-texts.com/chr/seil/seil82.htm.

2. Usually a man is appointed as "Spiritual Director" for other men, and a woman for other women. This guidance and instruction and counseling may take place during an intensive week during a live-in stay at a monastery—as a "retreat"—or during visits to a local church or even in one's home; such visits may be spread out over a month. The Spiritual Director *often becomes a close friend* of the student, *so close* that students are even urged and led to **CONFESS sins**, shortcomings, and problems—even when the Director is not a priest and the student is not a Roman Catholic.

3. An abbot is the head of the monks in a monastery called an abbey.

4. Thomas Keating, *Open Mind, Open Heart* (Amity, NY: Amity House, 1986), p. 97.

5. William Shakespeare, *Romeo and Juliet,* Act II, Scene ii, Line 33.

6. Sanskrit translation provided by Swami Rama, *Freedom From the Bondage of Karma* (Honesdale, PA: Himalayan Institute Press, 1977), p. 66.

7. Ray Yungen, *A Time of Departing,* Second Edition (Eureka, MT: Lighthouse Trails Publishing, 2006), pp. 15–16. Readers who wish to dig deeper into this heresy will find Yungen's well-researched book quite helpful, as I did.

8. Paul T. Harris, "Silent Teaching: The Life of Dom John Main," *Spirituality Today* (Winter 1988, vol. 40, no. 4), pp. 320–332; http://www.spiritualitytoday.org /spir2day/884043harris.html#6. See also: "Lives of the Heart and Soul," *Maclean's* magazine, September 14, 1987, p. 14.

9. Richard Foster and Emilie Griffin, *Spiritual Classics* (San Francisco, CA: Harper Collins, 2000), p. 155.

10. Harris, "Silent Teaching: The Life of Dom John Main."

11. *The Cloud of Unknowing: The Classic of Medieval Mysticism,* ed. Evelyn Underhill (Mineola, NY: Dover Publications, 2003), quoted by Yungen, *A Time of Departing,* p. 33.

12. Willigis Jager, *Contemplation: A Christian Path* (Ligouri, MO: Triumph Books, 1994), p. 31.

13. Henri Nouwen, *The Way of the Heart* (San Francisco, CA: Harper, 1991), p. 81.

14. J. P. Moreland and Klaus Issler, *The Lost Virtue of Happiness: Discovering the Disciplines of the Good Life* (Colorado Springs, CO: NavPress, 2006), pp. 90, 92–93.

15. Roger Oakland, *Faith Undone* (Silverton, OR: Lighthouse Trails Publishing, 2007), p. 119.
16. Richard J. Foster, *Prayer: Finding the Heart's True Home* (San Francisco, CA: Harper, 1992), p. 122.
17. Yungen, *A Time for Departing*, p. 75.
18. Tricia Rhodes, *The Soul at Rest: A Journey Into Contemplative Prayer* (Minneapolis, MN: Bethany House Publishers, 1996), p. 28.
19. William Johnston, *Letters to Contemplatives* (Maryknoll, NY: Orbis Books, 1992), p. 13.
20. Anthony de Mello, *Sadhana: A Way to God* (St. Louis: The Institute of Jesuit Resources, 1978), p. 28.
21. Foster, *Prayer: Finding the Heart's True Home*, p. 155.
22. Richard J. Foster, *Celebration of Discipline: The Path to Spiritual Growth*, Revised Edition (San Francisco, CA: Harper & Row, 1988), p. 103.
23. Basil Pennington, *Centering Prayer* (Garden City, NY: Image Books, 1982).
24. Keating, *Open Mind, Open Heart*, p. 114.
25. John D. Dreher, "The Danger of Centering Prayer," *This Rock* (November 1997), pp. 14–16, http://www.catholiceducation.org/articles/apologetics/ap0005.html.
26. Jacquelyn Small, *Awakening in Time* (New York: Bantam Books, 1991), p. 261.
27. Marcia Montenegro's, "Out of Your Mind: Meditation and Visualization," p. 2, on her CANA Web site: http://www.christiananswersforthenewage.org/Articles_Meditation.html.
28. Sybil Leek, *The Sybil Leek Book of Fortune-telling* (New York: Macmillan, 1969), p. 122.
29. Beth Moore, *Be Still* DVD (20th Century Fox, 2006).
30. Brother Lawrence, *The Practice of the Presence of God*, trans. John Delaney (Garden City, NY: Image Books, 1977), p. 34.
31. Beth Moore, *When Godly People Do Ungodly Things* (Nashville, TN: Broadman and Holman, 2002), p. 109.
32. Brennan Manning, *The Signature of Jesus* (Sisters, OR: Multnomah Books, 1996), p. 212.
33. Ibid., p. 218.
34. Ibid., p. 215.
35. See Matthew 8:24–27; Mark 4:37–41; Luke 8:23–25.
36. *Matthew Henry's Commentary on the Whole Bible: Complete and Unabridged* (Peabody, MA: Hendrickson Publishers, 1991), p. 810, on Psalm 46:10. Matthew Henry (1662–1714) was a Presbyterian minister and Bible scholar whose monumental *Commentary* was acclaimed in his time and remains popular today.
37. In his book *Prayer: Finding the Heart's True Home,* p. 149, Richard Foster writes: "So many passages of Scripture provide a touchstone for Meditative Prayer: 'Be still and know that I am God'; 'Abide in My love'; 'I am the Good Shepherd'; 'Rejoice in the Lord always.' " We've just finished examining the first one Foster listed and found that the battle-scene context offers no support for mystic-mantra prayer. And *neither do* **ANY** *of the other three* Foster listed—examine them for yourself and see if you agree that, although they're perfectly good Bible verses, they have absolutely **NO**

bearing on the subject of Contemplative Prayer. Foster, an acknowledged expert on that topic, claimed there are **"so many"** supportive passages of Scripture that apparently he had to shorten the list. But those that he allowed to remain make it look as if proponents of *MYSTICISM* are indeed "clutching at straws"!

38. Kenneth L. Woodward, "Talking to God," *Newsweek,* January 6, 1992, p. 44.

39. Thomas Keating gave this "LECTURE AND MEDITATIVE SESSION" on May 22, 2005, at The Falls Church (a conservative Episcopal Church that in late 2007 broke away, with sister churches, from the Episcopal Church USA), in Falls Church, Virginia. Marcia Montenegro's ministry is "Christian Answers for the New Age" or CANA. Her Web site address is: http://christiananswersforthenewage.org/.

40. A respected dictionary of biblical Greek tells us: "The term translated *room* refers to the inner room of a house, normally *without* any windows opening outside, the most private location possible (BDAG 988)." Footnote on Matthew 6:6 from the NET Bible online.

41. See Matthew 6:9–13.

42. Keating, *Open Mind, Open Heart,* p. 35. Keating *also* tells his followers to let all **feelings** go! But to do this, one would have to let go of any sentiments of LOVE or TRUST toward Jesus and our heavenly Father.

43. Matthew 22:37. See also Mark 12:30 and Luke 10:27–28.

44. Daniel Goleman, *The Meditative Mind* (Los Angeles: Tarcher / Putnam, Inc., 1988), p. 53.

45. Dreher, "The Danger of Centering Prayer," pp. 14–16.

46. **DEFINITION: Spiritual disciplines** = A set of practices in which believers might engage in order to have "a closer walk with God." **NOTE:** Someone who feels we're being too harsh on Contemplative Prayer may reasonably ask: *"What's **WRONG** with spiritual disciplines?"* The answer is that, while there's *nothing* "wrong" with such **good** and **acceptable** practices as fasting, prayer, and performing service for others, *it's **RARE,** if ever,* that when the "spiritual disciplines" are taught they do not <u>include</u> the discipline of "the Silence." Therefore, when the term "spiritual disciplines" is used, **mystic meditation** is almost always **smuggled in** by incorporating Contemplative Prayer. It's simply another tricky case of "Switching Labels." (For this insight I'm indebted to Ray Yungen, *A Time of Departing,* p. 206.)

47. http://en.wikipedia.org/wiki/Spiritual_Exercises_of_Ignatius_of_Loyola.

48. Thomas Merton, quoted in Rob Baker and Gray Henry, eds., *Merton and Sufism* (Louisville, KY: Fons Vitae, 1999), p. 41.

49. Henri Nouwen, *Thomas Merton, Contemplative Critic* (San Francisco, CA: Harper & Row Publishers, 1981), p. 28.

50. William Shannon, *Silent Lamp: The Thomas Merton Story* (New York: Crossroad Publishing Company, 1992), p. 276.

51. Yungen, *A Time of Departing,* p. 58

52. Foster and Griffen, *Spiritual Classics,* p. 17.

53. Thomas Keating, *Intimacy With God* (New York: Crossroad Publishing, 1994), p. 15.

54. Dreher, "The Danger of Centering Prayer," pp. 14–16.

55. Yungen, *A Time of Departing,* p. 61.

56. Michael Ford, *Wounded Prophet: A Portrait of Henri Nouwen* (New York: Doubleday, 1999), p. 35.

57. Rick Warren quoting Kay Warren on the Ministry Toolbox (Issue no. 54, June 5, 2002), http://www.pastors.com/RWMT/?ID=54.

58. Henri Nouwen, *In the Name of Jesus* (New York: Crossroad Publishing, 2000), pp. 6, 31–32.

59. In Galatians 1:6–9, the apostle Paul pronounces God's **curse** on any—even an angel!—who would dare to presume to **change** the teachings of His holy Word. Read it for yourself: "I marvel that you are turning away so soon . . . to a different gospel, which is not another [for Christ has *only ONE genuine* gospel]; but there are some who trouble you and want to *pervert* the gospel of Christ. But even if *we [that is, we apostles ourselves]*, or an *angel from heaven,* preach *any other* gospel to you than what we have preached to you, let him be *accursed.* As we have said before, so now I say again, if *anyone* preaches *any other* gospel to you than what you have received, let him be *accursed."*

60. Brennan Manning, *Above All* (Brentwood, TN: Integrity Publishers, 2003), pp. 58–59.

61. Philip Yancey, quoted in Brennan Manning, *Reflections for Ragamuffins* (San Francisco, CA: Harper, 1998), back cover.

62. James Sundquist, "Brennan Manning, Featured Speaker," *Christianity Today,* June 24, 2007.

63. Reginald A. Ray, "Religion Without God," *Shambhala Sun* (July 2001), http://www.shambhalasun.com/index.php?option=com_content&task=view&id=2233.

64. Thomas Keating, Basil Pennington, and Thomas E. Clarke, *Finding Grace at the Center* (Petersham, MA: St. Bede's Publications, 1978), pp. 5–6.

65. Keating, *Open Mind, Open Heart,* p. 127.

66. Johnnette Benkovic, *The New Age Counterfeit* (Grandview, TX: Faith Publishing Company, 1997), pp. 10–11.

67. Thomas Keating, quoted in Philip St. Romain, *Kundalini Energy and Christian Spirituality* (New York: Crossroad Publishers, 1991), Foreword.

68. Henri Nouwen, in the Foreword to Thomas Ryan, *Disciplines for Christian Living* (Mahwah, NJ: Paulist Press, 1993), pp. 2–3.

69. Thomas Merton, *The Springs of Contemplation* (New York: Farrar, Straus, Giroux, 1992), p. 266. Quoted also in Baker and Henry, eds., *Merton and Sufism,* p. 69.

70. **Definition:** "**Zen Buddhism** - noun - A Chinese and Japanese school of Mahayana Buddhism that asserts that **enlightenment** *can be attained through* **meditation, self-contemplation,** *and* **intuition** *rather than through* **scriptures**." *The American Heritage Dictionary,* Second College Edition (Boston: Houghton Mifflin Company, 1985), entry: "Zen Buddhism."

71. Foster and Griffin, eds., *Spiritual Classics,* p. 17.

72. Thomas Merton, quoted in Shannon, *Silent Lamp,* p. 276.

73. Brother Patrick Hart, ed., *The Message of Thomas Merton* (Kalamazoo, MI: Cistercian Publications, 1981) p. 63.

74. Thomas Merton, quoted in Frank X. Tuoti, *The Dawn of the Mystical Age* (New York: Crossroad Publishing Co., 1997), p. 127.

75. Thomas Merton, quoted in David Stendl-Rast, "Recollection of Thomas Merton's Last Days in the West," *Monastic Studies* (vol. 7, no. 10), 1969.
76. Richard J. Foster, *Celebration of Discipline: The Path to Spiritual Growth* (San Francisco: Harper & Row, 1978), p. 14.
77. Ibid., p. 170.
78. Foster, *Celebration of Discipline,* p. 94, footnote. **NOTE:** If you Google the LIBRARY OF CONGRESS CATALOG on the Internet, you'll find that this is the title Doherty gave her book: Catherine de Hueck Doherty, *Poustinia: Christian Spirituality of the East for Western Man* (Notre Dame, IN: Ave Maria Press, 1975). But she died in 1985, and if you look it up on AMAZON, you'll see that in its later 2000 edition her book's subtitle has been *changed* to read, Catherine de Hueck Doherty, *Poustinia: Encountering God in Silence, Solitude, and Prayer* (Washington, D.C.: Madonna House Publications, 2000). So what are they trying to hide from us? Incidentally, two years after she first published *Poustinia,* Doherty came out with *Sobornost: Eastern Unity of Mind and Heart for Western Man* (Notre Dame, IN: Ave Maria Press, 1977). It looks as if she, like Foster and Merton, was passionately dedicated to the same mission or crusade as other enthusiasts—that is, to spread *the religions of the East* to our Western minds.
79. Tilden Edwards, *Spiritual Friend* (New York: Paulist Press, 1980), p. 18. Dr. Edwards himself makes no attempt to hide his liberal, interspiritual approach to Christianity. One example was a workshop he did titled *Buddhist Contributions to Christian Living.*
80. The U.S. District Court, Newark, New Jersey, on October 29, 1977, and the U.S. Court of Appeals, Philadelphia, PA, on February 2, 1979. See "U.S. Court of Appeals Rules Against TM Movement," *Spiritual Counterfeits Project* (February 6, 1979).
81. Finbarr Flanagan, "Centering Prayer: Transcendental Meditation for the Christian Market," *Faith and Renewal* (May / June, 1991), p. 2. Quoted in Margaret Anne Feaster, "A Closer Look at Centering Prayer," http://www.catholicculture.org/culture/library/view.cfm?id=6337&CFID= 28668508&CFTOKEN=96653795.
82. THE TRANSCENDENTAL MEDITATION PROGRAM, http://www.tm.org/meditation -techniques.
83. John Main, quoted in Paul T. Harris, "Silent Teaching: The Life of Dom John Main," pp. 320–332.
84. Thomas Keating, *Open Mind, Open Heart,* Twentieth Anniversary Edition (New York: Continuum International Publishing Group, 2006), p. 23.
85. Jerry Alder, "In Search of the Spiritual," *Newsweek,* September 2005, p. 44, a Special Report seventeen pages long titled "Spirituality in America."
86. Thomas Keating, Basil Pennington, and Thomas Clarke, *Finding Grace at the Center* (Still River, MA: St. Bede's Publications, 1978), p. 20.
87. Basil Pennington, *Centering Prayer* (Garden City, NY: Doubleday Image Books, 1980), p. 234.
88. *Catechism of the Catholic Church* (New York: Doubleday Image Books, 1995), p. 717, Paragraph 2726.
89. Critics may point out that **Eastern** mystical methods use the names of their **pagan** gods for their mantras—as does TM—whereas CP uses **Christian** sacred words, such as "Jesus" or "Father" or similar names. But this is a *minor detail* compared with

the fact that **ALL** these mystical practices use a **MANTRA** to still the mind—just as their **NOT CALLING** the *mantra* that but choosing to call it a "prayer word" is *another minor detail.* It doesn't matter to ***devilish demons*** WHAT we *call* it—OR what word we *use*. The fallen angels we call demons are the very **embodiment** of EVIL, cruelly willing to lie, cheat, torture, and kill—if given the chance. So let's not fool ourselves: *None of the demons* honor God or revere His name, so they won't care much what word is used by those willing to disrespect God's Word enough to place themselves under Satan's demonic power.

90. Vijay Eswaran, *In the Sphere of Silence* (RYTHM House, 2005), http://www.inthesphereofsilence.com/

91. Quaker Web site for this quotation is http://quakerinfo.com/foster.shtml.

92. Some general differences are that Quaker churches *do not celebrate Easter or Christmas* in any religious way, they *do not celebrate the Lord's Supper,* they *do not practice any mode of water baptism,* and most of their churches have *no clergy.*

93. For those who desire more information about the Quakers, two excellent sources give fair and unbiased facts with plenty of details on almost every aspect of that religion. One is the **British Broadcasting Corporation** (the **BBC**) Web site: http://www.bbc.co.uk/religion/religions/christianity/subdivisions/quakers_1.shtml. Another is the **Ontario Consultants on Religious Tolerance** (the **OCRT**) Website: http://www.religioustolerance.org/quaker2.htm

94. Rosemary Guiley, *Harper's Encyclopedia of Mystical and Paranormal Experience* (San Francisco, CA: Harper, 1991), p. 556.

95. Young Mary Baker Eddy, who later founded Christian Science, had the SAME negative reaction to John Calvin's teaching that ALL humans are *already* "predestined" by God either for heaven or hell—*no matter* **how** they live or **what** they do, good or bad. She consequently started her own religion, and so did George Fox.

96. Kenneth Scott Latourette, *A History of Christianity: Reformation to the Present* (New York: Harper & Row, 1975), vol. 2, p. 882.

97. Latourette, *A History of Christianity,* p. 981.

98. Ken Silva, "Who Is Richard Foster?" *Apprising Ministries* (May 30, 2008), http://apprising.org/2008/05/30/who-is-richard-foster/.

99. Earle Cairns, *Christianity Through the Centuries* (Grand Rapids, MI: Zondervan, 1996), p. 381.

100. On the *Christianity Today* Web site: http://www.christianitytoday.com/ct/2008/september/26.41.html?start=1.

101. The late Pastor Adrian Rogers, quoted in Rick Warren, *The Purpose-Driven Church* (Grand Rapids, MI: Zondervan, 1995), Front Matter.

102. Warren, *The Purpose-Driven Church*, pp. 126–127.

103. Yungen, *A Time for Departing,* p. 143.

104. God's archenemy, Satan, knows he *already* has *the Christless religions* of the East and the New Age in his devilish grasp. But now, in this "pull out all the stops" attempt to capture **ALL** *of Christianity,* he is spreading Contemplative Prayer—a strategy admirably designed for just such a task. For Thomas Merton truly observed that "Contemplative consciousness is a **trans-cultural, trans-religious, trans-formed**

consciousness. . . . It can shine through *this* or *that* system, *religious* or *IR*religious." Thomas Merton, *Thoughts on the East* (New York: New Directions Books, 1995), p. 34.

105. Dan Kimball, *The Emerging Church: Vintage Christianity for New Generations* (Grand Rapids, MI: Zondervan, 2003), p. 60.

106. Ibid.

107. Robert Webber, *Ancient-Future Faith* (Grand Rapids, MI: Baker Books, 1999), pp. 135.

108. Ibid., p. 85.

109. Kimball, *The Emerging Church*, p. 169.

110. Roger Oakland, *Faith Undone* (Silverton, OR: Lighthouse Trails Publishing, 2008), p. 17.

111. Ibid., p. 18.

112. 2 Timothy 3:7, KJV.

113. Kimball, *The Emerging Church*, p. 136.

114. Julie B. Sevig, "Ancient New," *The Lutheran* (September 2001).

115. Oakland, *Faith Undone*, p. 60.

116. Kimball, *The Emerging Church*, p. 12.

117. Brian McLaren, *A New Kind of Christian* (San Francisco, CA: Jossey-Bass, 2001), p. xvi.

118. Brian McLaren, *A Generous Orthodoxy* (Grand Rapids, MI: Zondervan, 2004).

119. Oakland, *Faith Undone*, pp. 40–41.

120. Phyllis Tickle, *The Great Emergence* (Grand Rapids, MI: Baker Books, 2008), p. 164, footnote 7.

121. Mark Dyer, quoted in Tickle, *The Great Emergence*, p. 16.

122. Brian McLaren, *The Church on the Other Side* (Grand Rapids, MI: Zondervan, 2003), p. 68.

123. Marcia Montenegro, "Lecture and Meditation Session by Thomas Keating," http://www.christiananswersforthenewage.org/Articles_KeatingLecture.html.

124. See Luke 15:11–32.

125. Yungen, *A Time of Departing*, Second Edition, p. 87.

126. Rodney R. Romney, *Journey to Inner Space* (New York: Riverview Press, 1986), p. 132.

127. See Matthew 25:31–46; also, for example: John 5:28–29; Daniel 12:10; Matthew 13:24–30, 36–43.

128. Romney, *Journey to Inner Space*, p. 138.

129. A few examples may suffice: **Exodus 3:1–23**—God spoke to Moses from the blazing phenomenon of the burning bush, and they carried on an *audible* conversation at some length. **Acts 9:1–7**—The risen Jesus Christ spoke from heaven to the persecutor Saul (soon to be the apostle Paul) who not only saw "a light from heaven" but "heard a voice" and replied to it on the road to Damascus. This exchange was *audible, not silent,* for Paul's men "stood speechless, *hearing a voice,* but seeing no one" (**verse 7**). Countless other proofs like the angel Gabriel conversing with the Virgin Mary in **Luke 1:26–38**; as he did also with Zacharias (John the Baptist's father) in **Luke 1:5–25, 57–80**; *etc.,* may be cited.

130. Yungen, *A Time of Departing*, p. 88.

131. "*Vibrationally* sympathetic" refers to a person who is consensually willing, that is, willing to **consent** to listen to the spirit, as the "Hippies" of the New Age in the 1970s used to sing the praises of *"**good vibrations!**"*

132. Ken Carey, *The Starseed Transmissions* (Kansas City, MO: A Uni-Sun, 1985), p. 33.

133. The demons ought to know they're on the losing side, for they can never win against Almighty God. But still, even in Revelation 20:7–9—at almost the very end of the Bible—Satan foolishly gathers an army, without number, of ALL his devils and demons, _plus_ ALL the unsaved wicked who have ever lived but who have been resurrected by God to face judgment. In one last desperate attempt, the devil orders an attack on God's "beloved city, the New Jerusalem"—Revelation 3:12. All this, of course, is in vain, because John saw that *"fire* came down from God out of heaven, and _devoured_ them"—Revelation 20:9.

134. Ken Kaisch, *Finding God: A Handbook of Christian Meditation* (Mahwah, NJ: Paulist Press, 1994), pp. 63–64.

135. Leonard Sweet, *Quantum Spirituality* (Dayton, OH: Whaleprints, 1991), p. 76.

136. Calvin Miller, *Into the Depths of God* (Bloomington, MN: Bethany House Publishers, 2000), p. 96.

137. Thomas Merton, quoted in Yungen, *A Time of Departing,* p. 186.

138. Please read the whole inspiring passage in John 20:24–29.

139. Foster, *Celebration of Discipline,* p. 27.

140. Ibid., p. 26.

141. Rick Howard, *The Omega Rebellion* (Coldwater, MI: Remnant Publications, 2010), pp. 50–52.

142. See, for example, **Deuteronomy 18:9–12:** "When you come into the land which the Lord your God is giving you [that is, "the Promised Land"], you shall not learn to follow the **abominations** of those nations [the wickedly evil Canaanite nations]. There shall not be found among you anyone who **makes his son or his daughter pass through the fire,** or one who practices **witchcraft,** or a **soothsayer,** or one who **interprets omens,** or a **sorcerer,** or one who **conjures spells,** or a **medium,** or a **spiritist** [that is, a "**channeler**"], or one who **calls up the dead** [in a séance]. For **ALL** who do these things are an **abomination** to the Lord, and because of these **abominations** the Lord your God drives them out from before you." And disobedient King Saul was punished by death for his blatant transgression of consulting "the **witch** of Endor" (see **1 Samuel 28:3–25**) when he knew God had absolutely forbidden such a thing: "**So Saul died** for his unfaithfulness which he had committed against the Lord, because *he did not keep the word of the Lord, and also because he consulted a medium [a witch] for guidance." —***1 Chronicles 10:13**. The Lord of love makes these strong prohibitions against all these mystical, spiritualistic "**abominations**" _in order to protect us_ from the powers of the devil, for He knows that Satan and his demons are behind all such diabolical practices. For a penetrating look at King Saul's visit to the witch of Endor, see my book *Seven Mysteries Solved,* Second Edition, Revised (Fallbrook, CA: Hart Research Center, 2002), pp. 310–315—a biblical analysis which proves Saul was *deceived* by this clever counterfeit staged by Satan.

143. Foster, *Celebration of Discipline,* p. 16.

144. Willigis Jager, *Contemplation: A Christian Path* (Ligouri, MO: Triumph Books, 1994), p. 72.

145. Oakland, *Faith Undone,* p. 100.

146. David Hazard, in the "Introduction" to Bruce Demarest, *Satisfy Your Soul* (Colorado Springs, CO: NavPress, 1999), p. 18.

147. Ibid., pp. 37–38.

148. Benedicta Ward, *The Sayings of the Desert Fathers: The Alphabetical Collection,* translated from the Greek (London: Mowbrays, 1975).

149. Foster, *Celebration of Discipline,* p. 13.

150. Richard J. Foster, *Prayer: Finding the Heart's True Home* (San Francisco, CA: Harper, 1992), pp. 155–157. Jesus, in teaching "The Lord's Prayer," said: "Deliver us from evil." But this was asking God to guard us from Satan's schemes—*NOT a formula for warding off "all dark and evil spirits" <u>while we wordlessly, silently "pray"</u>*!

151. Brian Flynn, *Running Against the Wind: The Transformation of a New Age Medium and His Warning to the Church,* Second Edition (Silverton, OR: Lighthouse Trails Publishing, 2005), p. 145.

152. YOUTH SPECIALTIES is, unfortunately, today's leading youth ministry serving the Christian church. Each year it hosts dozens of well-attended youth congresses, weekend retreats, and workshops for youth themselves—and for training young pastors who are church youth leaders! Well-funded, it won a grant in 1997 from Lilly Endowment and has since been acquired by the giant religious publisher Zondervan. It prints *tons* of very attractive literature and features leading contemplative speakers at its assemblies. But its agenda is exclusively mystically oriented and has at its heart Contemplative Prayer. YOUTH SPECIALTIES is a spiritual "pied piper" leading our precious youth down a dangerous, mystical path.

153. Mike Perschon, "Desert Youth Worker: Disciplines, Mystics, and the Contemplative Life," *Youthworker* (November/December 2004), http://www.youthspecialties.com/articles/topics/spirituality/desert.php

154. Yungen, *A Time of Departing,* p. 176.

155. Laurie Cabot, *Power of the Witch* (New York: Bantam Doubleday Dell Publishing, 1989), p. 173.

156. Ibid., pp. 183 and 200.

157. 1 Timothy 4:1, KJV.

158. Thomas Keating, *Open Mind, Open Heart* (Amity, NY: Amity House, 1986), p. 15.

159. Thomas Keating, *Invitation to Love: The Way of Christian Contemplation* (Rockport, MA: Element, 1992), p. 129.

160. Benkovic, *The New Age Counterfeit,* p. 23–24.

161. Peter Thomas Rohrbach, *Conversation With Christ,* by St. Teresa of Avila (Rockford, IL: Tan Publishing Co.) p. 78.

162. Cardinal Joseph Ratzinger, *Letter to the Bishops of the Catholic Church on Some Aspects of Christian Meditation,* Oct. 15, 1989, from the English version, p. 34, footnote 12. And Pope John Paul II, *Homilia Abulae habita in honorem Sanctae Teresiae*: AAS 75 (1983), pp. 256–257.

163. *Cathechism of the Catholic Church* (New York: Doubleday, 1995), paragraph 2726. Italics were used for emphasis in the original warning.

164. Brennan Manning, *The Ragamuffin Gospel: Good News for the Bedraggled, Beat-up, and Burnt Out* (Portland, OR: Multnomah, 1990), p. 21.

165. See Winfried Corduan, *Mysticism, an Evangelical Option?* (Grand Rapids, MI: Zondervan, 1991), p. 120. See also Gary Gilley at http://www.svchapel.org/resources /articles/23-doctrine/547-mysticism-part-3.

166. Foster, *Celebration of Discipline*, p. 17.

167. Foster, *Prayer: Finding the Heart's True Home*, p. 160.

168. Brennan Manning, *The Signature of Jesus*, Revised Edition (Sisters, OR: Multnomah, 1996) pp. 188–189.

169. David Cloud, "Beware of Brennan Manning," *Way of Life Literature*, http://www .wayoflife.org/files/9ad06042d49138696773e1f9849f1aff-144.html.

170. Brennan Manning, *The Ragamuffin Gospel*, p. 14.

171. Ibid., p. 171.

172. Revelation 19:16.

173. Rick Warren's Ministry Toolbox (September 3, 2003 and February 18, 2004).

174. Tricia Rhodes, *The Soul at Rest: A Journey Into Contemplative Prayer* (Minneapolis, MN: Bethany House Publishers, 1996), p. 199.

175. Ibid., p. 55.

176. Rick Warren, *The Purpose-Driven Life* (Grand Rapids, Michigan: Zondervan, 2002), pp. 285–286.

177. Oakland, *Faith Undone*, p. 155. Furthermore, *in the very passage* Rick Warren mutilates, our Lord Jesus specifically mentions **"Daniel the prophet,"** which His disciples are told to "understand"—implying reading and study (**Matthew 24:15**).

178. In our survey of various communities of faith in this book, we've seen that some have their own special scriptures. The *world* religions of Hinduism, Buddhism, Judaism, and Islam each have their own exclusive scriptures because they consider *different texts* sacred, inspired, and holy, and also because their adherents speak *different languages*. But only a *FEW* of the English-speaking denominations have their own "Bibles." We can easily count them on the fingers of one hand—just three: **Christian Science** *(Science and Health with Key to the Scriptures);* **Mormonism** *(Book of Mormon, Doctrine and Covenants,* and *The Pearl of Great Price)*; **Jehovah's Witnesses** *(New World Translation).* **Roman Catholics**, of course, have the Douay and the Jerusalem Bible *versions,* but not completely different Bibles. All the other many Christian churches seem to find their doctrines, their teachings and beliefs, within the pages of the Old and New Testaments which we call the Bible. That's why it seems quite strange that Richard Foster and his own chosen few have felt the need to produce their *private version* of God's holy Word—an *English* Bible with a *foreign* name, the *Renovaré Spiritual Formation Bible. Renovaré* is a French word for "renewal."

179. "A Conversation with Eugene Peterson," *Mars Hill Review* (Fall 1995, Issue no. 3), pp. 73–90.

180. 2 Timothy 2:15; 3:16–17, KJV.

181. Richard J. Foster, *Celebration of Discipline*, Revised Edition (San Francisco: Harper San Francisco, 1988), p. 19.

182. Yungen, *A Time of Departing*, Second Edition, p. 52. Matthew 7:13–14 is quoted here from the New Living Translation.

183. 1 Corinthians 1:18.

184. Henri Nouwen, *Bread for the Journey* (San Francisco, CA: Harper, 1997), daily readings for January 15 and November 16.

185. Henri Nouwen, *Here and Now* (New York: Crossroad Publishing Co., 1994), p. 22.

186. John R. Yungblut, *Rediscovering the Christ* (Rockport, MA: Element Books, 1991), p. 142.

187. Malachi Martin, *The Jesuits: The Society of Jesus and the Betrayal of the Roman Catholic Church* (New York: Simon & Schuster, 1987), pp. 206–207.

188. Matthew 6:9, KJV. Other explicit verses echo the same thought. Psalm 11:4 says, "The Lord is in His holy Temple, the Lord's throne is in Heaven."

189. Yungen, *A Time of Departing*, p. 108.

190. Genesis 3:5.

191. Basil Pennington, *Awake in the Spirit: A Personal Handbook on Prayer* (New York: Crossroad Publishing Company, 1992), p. 81.

192. Matthew Fox, *The Coming of the Cosmic Christ* (New York: HarperCollins Publishers, 1988), p. 154.

193. Ibid., p. 232.

194. Thomas Merton, quoted in Henri Nouwen, *Thomas Merton: Contemplative Critic* (San Francisco, CA: Harper & Row, Publishers, 1991), pp. 46, 71.

195. Brother Patrick Hart, ed., *The Message of Thomas Merton* (Kalamazoo, MI: Cistercian Publications, 1981) p. 200. Italics are in the original for emphasis.

196. Beatrice Bruteau, in "A Song That Goes On Singing: An Interview With Dr. Beatrice Bruteau," by Amy Edelstein and Ellen Daly in *Enlightenment Magazine,* Spring–Summer Issue, 2002. Quoted from http://www.lighthousetrailsresearch.com/manning.htm.

197. Exodus 3:13–14: "Then Moses said to God, 'Indeed, when I come to the children of Israel and say to them, "The God of your fathers has sent me to you," and they say to me, "What is His name?" what shall I say to them?' And God said to Moses, 'I AM WHO I AM.' And He said, 'Thus you shall say to the children of Israel, "I AM has sent me to you."'"

198. Sue Monk Kidd, *God's Joyful Surprise* (San Francisco, CA: Harper, 1987), pp. 55, 198.

199. Ibid., pp. 233, 228.

200. Ibid., pp. 228–229.

201. Sue Monk Kidd, *The Dance of the Dissident Daughter: A Woman's Journey From Christian Tradition to the Sacred Feminine* (San Francisco, CA: Harper Collins, 1996), pp. 162–163.

202. Yungen, *A Time of Departing*, p. 137.

203. Kidd, *The Dance of the Dissident Daughter,* p. 76.

204. See John 8:13, 44.

205. Matthew 23:13, NIV.

206. Acts 17:27.

207. Kidd, *The Dance of the Dissident Daughter,* pp. 161, 163.

208. Foster, *Celebration of Discipline,* p. 15.

209. Pastor Gary Gilley, "Contemplative Prayer—the Heart of Mysticism," *Mysticism – Part 3,* (March 2005, vol. 11, no. 3), on his Southern View Chapel Web site: http://www.svchapel.org/resources/articles/23-doctrine/547-mysticism-part-3.

210. Theophan the Recluse, quoted in Richard J. Foster, *Celebration of Discipline: The Path to Spiritual Growth*, Twentieth Anniversary Revised Edition (New York: Harper Collins, 1998), p. 19.
211. Madame Guyon, quoted in Willigis Jager, *The Search for the Meaning of Life* (Ligouri, MO: Ligouri/Triumph Books, 1995), p. 125.
212. Dr. Dean Ornish, *Dr. Dean Ornish's Program for Reversing Heart Disease* (New York: Ballantine Books, 1991), p, 247.
213. M. Scott Peck, *The Road Less Traveled* (New York: Simon & Schuster, 1978), p. 283.
214. M. Scott Peck, *Further Along the Road Less Traveled* (Simon & Schuster Audioworks, 1992).
215. Interview with M. Scott Peck, *New Age Journal* (December 1985), pp. 28–30.
216. M. Scott Peck, *A World Waiting to Be Born* (New York: Bantam Books, 1993), pp. 88–89.
217. Ibid., p. 83.
218. Richard Abanes and H. Wayne House, *The Less Traveled Road and the Bible: A Scriptural Critique of the Philosophy of M. Scott Peck* (Camp Hill, PA: Horizon Books, 1995), pp. 28–29.
219. Michael D'Antonio, *Heaven on Earth* (New York: Crown Publishing, 1992), pp. 342–352.
220. Robert Schuller, *Peace of Mind Through Possibility Thinking* (Garden City, NY: Doubleday, 1977), pp. 131–132. Quoted in Dave Hunt and T. A. McMahon, *The Seduction of Christianity* (Eugene, Oregon: Harvest House Publishers, 1985), p. 132.
221. Dave Hunt and T. A. McMahon, *The Seduction of Christianity* (Eugene, OR: Harvest House Publishers, 1985), p. 132.
222. Foster, *Be Still* DVD.
223. Yungen, *A Time of Departing*, p. 120.
224. Armand Biteaux, *The New Consciousness* (Willits, CA: Oliver Press, 1975), p. 128.
225. John Randolph Price, *The Planetary Commission* (Austin, TX: Quartus Books, 1984), pp. 143, 145.
226. Jager, *Contemplation: A Christian Path*, pp. 93–94.
227. 1 Timothy 4:1, KJV.
228. Henri Nouwen, *Bread for the Journey* (San Francisco, CA: Harper, 1997).
229. Yungen, *A Time of Departing*, p. 131.
230. Henri Nouwen, *Sabbatical Journey* (New York: Crossroad Publishing, 1998), p. 51.
231. John R. Yungblut, *Rediscovering the Christ* (Rockport, MA: Element Book, 1991), p. 164.
232. Thomas Merton, *Conjectures of a Guilty Bystander* (Garden City, NY: Doubleday, 1966), pp. 157–158.
233. Philip St. Romain, *Kundalini Energy and Christian Spirituality* (New York: Crossroad Publishing Company, 1995), p. 39. By the way, St. Romain should know this, but in case his spiritual directors haven't told him, the very title of his New Age book is an interesting paradox or oxymoron when linked with the word *Christian*. For the Sanskrit word *kundalin* means "coiled, like a snake." And in Hinduism *kundalini* is commonly referred to by masters of yoga as *the SERPENT POWER!*—so-called because Hindus believe *it lies like a coiled serpent* in the root *chakra* at the base of

our spine just waiting to be released. They are *deceptive* in trying to call the book *Christian Spirituality.* But in forthrightly labelling it "Serpent Power," at least they're "calling a spade a spade" and not trying to *switch labels* on us!

234. Adapted from Gary Gilley, "Contemplative Prayer, the Heart of Mysticism," *Mysticism – Part 3* (March 2005, vol. 11, no. 3), from his SOUTHERN VIEW CHAPEL Web site, http://www.svchapel.org/resources/articles/23-doctrine/547-mysticism-part-3.

235. John 17:17.

236. John 8:44.

237. Isaiah 40:8. Also, in Malachi 3:6, KJV, God says, "I am the Lord, *I change NOT.*" And Hebrews 13:8, KJV, declares "Jesus Christ the SAME *yesterday, and today, and for ever.*"

238. And the devil himself—Lucifer/Satan—is *also* mortal and therefore subject to death. The Bible says that God will bring that rebellious fallen angel "to **ASHES** . . . and **NEVER** shalt thou **BE** any more." —**Ezekiel 28:13–19**, KJV. For readers to whom this biblical truth is new, please see my book *Seven Mysteries Solved,* Second Edition, Revised (Fallbrook, CA: Hart Research Center, 2002), Chapter 12, "Eternal Torment: A Burning Issue," pp. 343–366.

239. Ephesians 5:11.

Meet the Author

Howard Peth was born in Chicago, Illinois, where he grew up—except for two carefree years spent in Fort Worth, Texas. He's lived his adult life in Southern California. With degrees from both UCLA and USC, he spent forty-two enjoyable years in the stimulating arena of the classroom, thirty-one of them at Mt. San Antonio College in Walnut, California, serving also as a department chairman.

Retiring recently to the San Diego area, Mr. Peth now spends much of his time writing and presenting screen-illustrated lectures. He and Diane, his wife of fifty-seven years, have three grown children and six grandchildren.